THROUGH
CHINESE EYES

About the Authors

Peter J. Seybolt has a Master of Arts in Teaching degree and a Ph.D. in History and East Asian Languages (Chinese and Japanese) from Harvard University. He has taught at both the high school and college level and is currently Professor of History at the University of Vermont. His publications include the books *Revolutionary Education in China, The Rustication of Urban Youth in China,* and *Language Reform in China* (with Gregory Kuei-ko Chiang). He is editor of the journal *Chinese Education,* and author of numerous journal articles, reviews and translations from Chinese.

Leon E. Clark, the author of *Through African Eyes,* is the general editor of the CITE World Culture Series. He received his B.A. and M.A. from Yale University and his doctorate in International Education from the University of Massachusetts. For the past fifteen years he has been involved in a variety of educational activities both within and outside the United States. He has been a high school and college teacher; Associate Director of the Social Sciences and Humanities Center, Teachers College, Columbia; and associate director of the Governmental Affairs Institute in Washington, D.C. He has also taught in the University of Mysore, India, conducted research in both India and Africa, and served as a consultant to several Asian and African nations. The author of several books and numerous articles on education and international affairs, Dr. Clark is presently on the faculty of American University in Washington, D.C.

THROUGH CHINESE EYES

Revolution and Transformation

PETER J. SEYBOLT

LEON E. CLARK, General Editor

A CITE BOOK

New York ● Washington

Published in the United States of America in 1988
by CITE Books
The Center for International Training and Education
777 United Nations Plaza, Suite 9-A
New York, NY 10017

Library of Congress Cataloging-in-Publication Data

Seybolt, Peter J.
    Through Chinese Eyes.

    "A CITE book."
    Summary: Introduces the sociology and recent history of China.
    1. China—History—1949—   . [1.China]
I. Clark, Leon E., 1935— . II. Title.
DS777.55.S454   1988   951   87-22427
ISBN 0938960-30-X
ISBN 0-938960-29-6 (pbk.)

For Cynthia, Taylor, and Amy

Acknowledgments

MANY PEOPLE HAVE contributed to this book. I am most indebted to my wife, Cynthia, who commented critically on the manuscript in its various stages of production and contributed significantly to its final form, and to Leon Clark, who suggested the project and spent many hours helping to bring it to fruition. Both the structure and the content of the book bear the imprint of his wise counsel and expert editing.

I have also benefited from discussions with Richard Minear, who was engaged in a similar project on Japan.

Numerous friends and colleagues have offered suggestions and aid which improved the manuscript. I would particularly like to thank Fred Drake and Donald Johnson for allowing me access to their excellent photograph collections, Stephen Bloom for contributing his time and technical skill in reproducing many of the photographs, and Carolyn Perry for doing much of the typing.

Finally, I would like to thank Claire Malcolm Lintilhac for her gentle advice and for sharing her rich insights derived from having lived for fifty years in China.

P.S.

Contents

Foreword

PEOPLE—AND NATIONS—have a tendency to look at the outside world from their own perspectives. This is natural and perhaps necessary, for we are all prisoners of a particular space and time. But how limited and boring one perspective can be! And how faulty and biased our information would be if we listened only to ourselves!

The main goal of THROUGH CHINESE EYES is to broaden our perspective by presenting a Chinese view of China and the world. Almost all of the material in this volume has been written by Chinese, and it has been taken from a variety of sources: autobiographies, fiction, poetry, newspaper and magazine articles, and historical documents.

Unlike most books about "other peoples," THROUGH CHINESE EYES does not try to *explain* China but to *show* it; it does not offer "expert" analysis by outside observers but, rather, attempts to recreate the reality of everyday life as experienced by the Chinese people. Interpretation is left to the reader. In effect, THROUGH CHINESE EYES has two objectives; to let the Chinese speak for themselves, and to let readers think for themselves.

This edition of THROUGH CHINESE EYES was originally published in two volumes. Volume 1 is presented here as Part I and Volume 2 as Part II.

Part I, *Revolution: A Nation Stands Up*, begins with the story of the Communist rise to power in 1949, which led to perhaps the most spectacular social revolution the world has ever seen—and it is still going on. In only a handful of years, the Communists have been able to transform the lives of one billion Chinese, almost one quarter of the world's population.

Part I focuses on the changes brought about in the lives of the peasants, the masses who make their living from the land. It also presents material on recent changes in family life, religion, women's roles and politics.

Part II, *Transformation: Building a New Society*, continues the theme of change by exploring the struggles and debates within China over economic development, the proper path for socialism, and the role of literature and art in society. It also examines such issues as population growth, pollution, health care, and China's foreign policy. It ends with a section on the Chinese American experience.

Historical material is interspersed throughout both parts, providing a glimpse of China's rich past and at the same time indicating the continuity and contrast with the present.

In some ways, China may seem different from the United States, and indeed it is. But in many more ways, the Chinese as people are similar to people anywhere in the world. Human beings, no matter where they live, face the same basic needs: to eat, to work, to love, to play, to get along with their fellow human beings. Learning how the Chinese respond to these needs may teach us something useful for our own lives.

More important, getting to know the Chinese as people—sharing in their thoughts and feelings, their beliefs and aspirations—should help us to develop a sense of empathy, a feeling of identity, with human beings everywhere. In the end we should know more about ourselves—indeed, we should have an expanded definition of who we are—because we will know more about the common humanity that all people share. Self-knowledge may be the ultimate justification for studying about other people.

LEON E. CLARK

Revolution
A Nation Stands Up

Introduction

. . . once China's destiny is in the hands of the Chinese people, China, like the rising sun in the east, will illuminate every corner of the land with a brilliant flame, swiftly clean up the mire left by the reactionary government, heal the wounds of war, and build a new, powerful people's republic worthy of the name.

Mao Tse-tung, June, 1949[*]

We have a common feeling that our work will be recorded in the history of mankind, and that it will clearly demonstrate that the Chinese, who comprise one quarter of humanity, have begun to stand up. . . .
  Henceforth our nation will enter the large family of peace-loving and freedom-loving nations of the world. . . . Our nation will never again be an insulted nation. We have stood up.

Mao Tse-tung, September, 1949[†]

Mao Tse-tung, Chairman of the Communist Party of China, uttered these words in 1949, shortly before the Communists established a new government called the People's Republic of China. Mao's words reveal a sense of destiny, an awareness that the Chinese revolution then taking place would have a profound impact not only on China but on the whole world.

---

[*] Mao Tse-tung, *Selected Works of Mao Tse-tung*, Vol. IV (Peking: Foreign Languages Press, 1961), p. 408.
[†] Stuart Schram, *The Political Thought of Mao Tse-tung* (New York: Praeger, 1969), p. 167.

Today we are only beginning to realize how prophetic his words were.

What did Mao Tse-tung mean when he said "China has stood up"? Stood up to whom? Why was China down? To appreciate the significance of this phrase we must have some knowledge of China's past.

For over two thousand years, until the late 1800's, the Chinese considered themselves the only truly civilized people on earth. They felt they needed nothing from the outside world and had nothing to learn from it.

Their sense of superiority was not empty self-delusion. Chinese poets and painters were at the height of their creative genius a thousand years ago, when Europe was in the Dark Ages and America was yet to be discovered by Europeans. The compass, gunpowder, and movable-type printing were all invented in China long before they were known in Europe.

These inventions, which played so great a part in the development of the modern West, changed almost nothing in China. In traditional China, harmony and stability were valued. Conflict and change were avoided. The idea of progress was unknown.

Secure in their sense of superiority and their self-sufficiency, the Chinese were blind to the changes taking place elsewhere in the world. Then, in 1840, the British defeated the Chinese in a war and imposed treaties on them that gave foreigners special rights in China and put them above Chinese law. A once superior people became inferior, discriminated against in their own country. China's system of government, which for two thousand years had provided a unity and stability unknown elsewhere in the world, rapidly disintegrated in the face of Western demands. The last Chinese emperor abdicated in 1911. Four decades of chaos followed. All attempts to build a new nation and to free China from foreign domination failed until 1949, when Mao Tse-tung and the Chinese Communist Party provided the leadership and inspiration that enabled China to "stand up."

For Mao and the Communists, standing up meant far

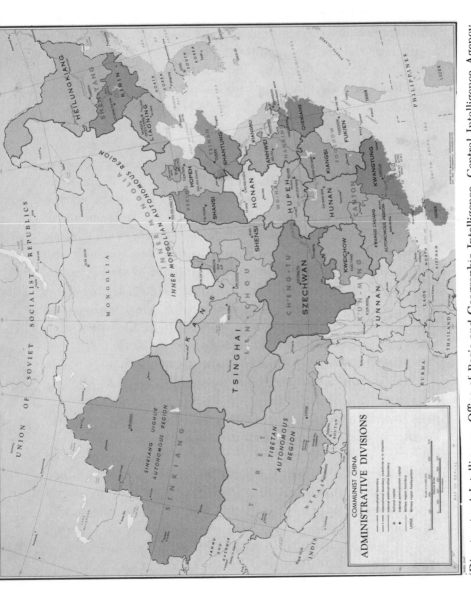

(Directorate of Intelligence, Office of Basic and Geographic Intelligence, Central Intelligence Agency, *Communist China Map Folio* [Washington: Central Intelligence Agency, 1967], n.p.)

more than casting off the weight of foreign oppression. It also meant casting off tradition, which for centuries had burdened the peasant farmer with an almost intolerable load. China stood up because the Chinese peasant stood up. Peasant revolution brought the Communists to power.

There is much to admire in traditional China. The appeal of Chinese art, literature, and philosophy is timeless and very broad. But let us not confuse the gems of a civilization with the daily life of the majority of the people. Until recently, most Chinese could not read, much less afford to own the exquisite jade ornaments or beautiful glazed porcelain ("china") that we associate with Chinese culture. For them life was a continual struggle for survival. The old ruling class, for all its accomplishments, had purchased the pleasures and refinements of high culture with the sweat of laboring people. Taxes, rents, and interest on loans provided the rich with their treasures and kept the worker and peasant on the threshold of starvation.

Finally, the pressures for change introduced by the West combined with long-standing grievances of the laboring poor to form an explosive mixture. "Maoism" was the spark that changed age-old peasant rebelliousness to revolution.

The Chinese revolution continues today, although not in the violent form it has sometimes assumed in the past. What is the nature of this revolution? What does it mean to the Chinese people? How has it changed their lives? This book will attempt to answer these questions and will raise others. As you study the Chinese experience, you should keep in mind that one of every four or five people in the world is Chinese. China is the most populous nation on earth and one of the largest geographically. What happens in China will inevitably influence the rest of the world in one way or another. As you read about China, think about your own life and your own society. How will changes in China affect you?

Lin-hsien County
From Poverty to Prosperity

Editor's Introduction: At least 80 per cent of the Chinese people live in the countryside. That is where the Chinese revolution began, and it is where the greatest changes have taken place. If you went to rural China today, what would you see? The report of a perceptive American journalist helps us make the transition from our own environment to that of China.

FOR AN AMERICAN, a drive deep into Lin-hsien County in the northwest corner of Honan Province is like driving straight into the early nineteenth or late eighteenth century.

It is threshing time in Lin-hsien County now—with a bumper crop of wheat—and all around one sees the broad threshing floors of hard-baked clay and hundreds of men and women and children winnowing the wheat, tossing it into the air with wooden shovels and letting the wind separate the grain from the chaff, just as Americans did before the days of the threshing machine.

And in the fields, men and women bowed to the waist stride swiftly through the high golden grain, cutting it with their scythes and quickly binding the sheaves with a strand of

Harrison E. Salisbury, "Once-Arid Region of China Blooms," *New York Times*, June 27, 1972. © 1972 by The New York Times Company. Reprinted by permission.

fiber, just as Americans did before the days of the McCormick reaper.

Beside the threshing floors rise great cones and cottages of straw, neat and orderly, enough for regiments of little pigs to live in. Some of the conical mounds of straw are already being covered with a heavy layer of clay, which will harden in the fierce Honan sunshine and create a mud silo that will preserve the straw for winter forage.

This is what you see as your car winds for 120 or 150 miles over the remote roads and tracks of Lin-hsien County.

There is an incredible bustle on the roads, cart after cart drawn by men or donkeys, or men and donkeys, or horses or occasionally cows, pulling everything the countryside can need. There is grain going to storage depots, cotton to gins, coal to steel mills or country brick-kilns, great truck tires from the Lin-hsien tire factory, iron pots for the villages, coke for the steel mill, limestone from local deposits, iron ore for the smelter, manure for the fields, and earth for bricks.

Whatever it is that mankind needs in Lin-hsien County, here it is in the carts. Even long after nightfall they go on, many of them with one or two great sails so that the wind can help the tireless donkey—or man—with his burden.

Here are more children than you have ever seen in a day. They line every village street, they peer from every courtyard entryway, they appear by the scores to look at the foreigners, they gather scrub oak leaves on the mountainsides to feed the wild silkworms, and they harrow the newly harvested fields to ready them for the second crop, which will be corn or sweet potatoes.

Men are pulling wooden plows through the brown clay soil, and cows are endlessly circling the wells to pump up the water. The houses are built of stone or adobe. . . . Women [are] visible at their hand looms and huge iron basins, each holding a meal for the great families—a dozen or fourteen members is not unusual.

The American sees all this and feels transported into the

past, although even in the American past it is doubtful that such a labor-intensive life ever could have existed.

But what does the Chinese see? Something entirely different—a countryside, Lin-hsien County, transformed beyond recognition.

This was an arid and barren countryside that traditionally had an exodus of population. There was drought nine years out of ten, and poor peasants traditionally sold their children and went out to beg to earn enough to escape starvation.

Chinese eyes see Lin-hsien County as a land of promise. Since the construction of an enormous canal to bring water from the Chang River, which divides Honan and Shansi provinces, life has changed amazingly. The canal was completed eight years ago, and it, together with other irrigation projects, enable the entire county to have water now.

The Honan people regard this as an accomplishment equivalent to the construction of the Great Wall of China. The canal is not so large as the Great Wall, but the comparison is not altogether out of place, for more than 21 million cubic yards of earth and stone were moved—enough to build a twelve-foot-wide highway from Canton in South China to Shen-yang in Manchuria.

Chinese eyes see healthy children. Cholera, smallpox, measles, venereal and other epidemic diseases have vanished. They see people who are lean and muscular from working from 5:30 A.M. to 10 or 11 P.M., but no undernourishment and no serious dietary diseases.

They see roads, . . . stony, dusty, bumpy, but genuine roads in place of the cart tracks and footpaths that connected most of these villages ten years ago. And they see the extraordinary rash of home-building.

American eyes can see that the country is fruitful and the people healthy. But Chinese eyes are needed to record the full measure of the change.

Lin-hsien County
A Recollection of the Past

&§*Editor's Introduction:* The previous article on Lin-hsien County concluded that "Chinese eyes are needed to record the full measure of change." Let us look at Lin-hsien County in the past through the eyes of a Chinese who lived there thirty years ago. His account is one of a collection of stories recalling the bitterness of the past. In recent years, the Communists have encouraged the publication of such stories to show young people in China how things have changed and to remind them that continued progress requires the same hard work and constant struggle that eliminated the misery once commonplace for much of the populace.

Not all landlords in China were as bad as Yang Chen-kang, the villain in the story, but there is no question that the landlord system fostered inequality of wealth and much suffering. The Communists define a landlord family as one that owned land but did no work. It lived by renting land to peasants, who often had to give the landlord as much as half of what they produced.

The Communists estimate that families of landlords and "rich peasants" (farmers who worked the land but had a surplus to rent out) were about 8 per cent of the rural population before 1949, and that they owned 80 per cent of the land. The other 92 per cent of the population were classed as "middle peasants" (those who could support themselves without renting land but had no excess

Yueh Feng and Wang Tien-ch'i, "The Land," *The People of T'ai-hang* (Peking: China Youth Publishing House, 1964). Translated in *Chinese Anthropology*, Vol. 4, No. 4 (New York: International Arts and Sciences Press, 1972), pp. 300–306; abridged. Used by permission.

land to rent out), "poor peasants" (those who owned land but not enough to support themselves and who had to rent land from others), and hired laborers, who owned no land at all. The story that follows is told by a former poor peasant. What political conditions, not mentioned in the story, had to exist to give the landlord so much power?ह≈

I WAS BORN in . . . Lin-hsien [County], Honan Province. As soon as I was able, I began to follow my mother to the fields. She went in front digging up the earth. I came behind breaking up the clods. Every day, by noon, my mother sat on the ground, so tired that she did not even want to eat. She only drank water in huge gulps. Usually, I massaged her back, waist, and legs. Once I asked her, "Why doesn't my father show up to help us till the land?" Immediately her eyelids reddened, and I never dared ask that question again.

Every time it rained there were leaks in our thatched roof. We were kept busy rolling up our mats and trying to prevent our pillows from getting wet, but nothing kept dry. In the confusion, my grandmother usually started complaining about my father. . . .

"I've told your husband a hundred times that he should find some time to repair the roof, but he won't listen! He is a farmhand employed on a regular basis, but he is not a slave of the Yangs. His father said as he was dying, 'Never hire out to the Yangs. Never fill the rice bowl of that house.' Ha! But he won't listen! Has he forgotten how his father died? The Yang house killed him with overwork and anger. And he went to his grave with nothing.

"Little Chin-pao, whenever you and your younger brother argue, remember what your grandfather said. Don't go to the Yang house. Don't fill the rice bowl of that house," said my grandmother, hugging my brother and me.

"Of the twenty or thirty families in this village, which one doesn't till the Yangs' land? If we don't till, what will we eat?" my mother asked.

"Does the rice of the Yang house taste so good? Sooner or later, bad things will happen!" my grandmother warned.

After it was all said, my grandmother began to weep, my mother began to weep, and my younger brother, Yin-ao, and I also began to weep. And that rain was still falling through our thatched roof.

Later, I was told that my ancestors had passed down two *mou* of land. [A *mou* is about one-sixth of an acre.] After the

Starving peasants in the 1930s. (Photo courtesy Jean Elliott Johnson.)

birth of my father and his two brothers, Grandfather could not support his family with the meager income from the crop on this small plot. Although he should never have done it, he leased several *mou* of land from the big landlord Yang Chen-kang. He worked hard, the suffering increased, and the back taxes accumulated into a large debt. Yang Chen-kang had the nickname of "Black Snake," and this venomous viper coiled around our family. He wanted to recover the debt by seizing our two *mou* of land. My grandfather could never give up that land, so he had to work for Yang Chen-kang and pay back his debt with his wages. He toiled for more than twenty years, but he was unable to clear the debt. When my grandfather died, we still had that two *mou* of land, which was still insufficient to feed us. Like my grandfather, my father leased a plot of land from Yang Chen-kang. The same things happened again. My father incurred a debt and had to work for Yang Chen-kang and repay his debt with his wages. And so we slaved for the Yang house from one generation to the next.

After the birth of my second younger brother, Ch'üan-pao, which meant another mouth to feed, my mother worried all the more. One night my father returned from work and stood by the *k'ang* and stared at me and my two brothers. He said: "One generation after another! Will they too have to lease land, run up debts, and forever be trampled under the feet of others?" My mother thought he looked strange and asked about it. But he would not say anything. At that time, my father often got together with some of his poor friends. Often he did not come back until midnight. We did not know what he was up to. As soon as someone called him from the yard, he hurried off. This added much to my mother's worries. She feared something would happen. . . .

Early on the morning of December 20, someone knocked at the door and cried: "Oh no, Chin-pao's father has been murdered!" Immediately, my mother pulled me and carried my younger brothers to the riverbank. Oh god! My father's body was there. . . .

Yang Chen-kang had said that he wanted to arrest the culprit, but in fact the culprit was Yang Chen-kang himself. My father and his friends had aroused his suspicion. He was fearful lest the poor people in the village unite against him. He decided to "show his strength by making the first move." In order to kill one to warn a hundred, he ordered one of his lackeys to murder my father. He also planned to seize our two *mou* of land.

When Grandmother heard this story, she grew both angry and vengeful. Her heart was overflowing with the death of her husband and her son, but she could not even tell the world. She lay on the *k'ang* mortally sick. She died a few days later.

My brothers and I helped Mother till our land. We worked from before dawn till after dusk. We were cultivating two plots of land: one was our own two *mou* of land; the other was the four *mou* of land that my father had leased from Yang Chen-kang. . . .

Who would have imagined that God himself would have his eyes closed to us? It did not rain for more than three months, and the wheat sprouts were becoming yellow and wasted. My mother's hopes for paying off our debt were crushed, and she fell sick from worry.

After the autumn harvest, Yang Chen-kang seized our two *mou* of land and took two large earthen vessels and a large wash basin away from us, which in no way diminished our debt. Yang Chen-kang also sent someone to fetch me back so that I could work for him as a shepherd and thereby work off our debt with my wages. My mother was infuriated and she swore at the man: "Black-hearted black snake! You taxed us for using a few *mou* of your land. You tortured my father-in-law to death. You murdered my husband. You seized our land. Now, you're going to lay your hands on my son!" She recalled my grandfather's words: Never make a living by filling the rice bowl of the Yang house. But if she did not send me, they would have no mercy. So, Mother finally sent me off to him with her tears. . . .

Stone Wall Village Turns Over

PART I

‹§*Editor's Introduction:* Changes in Lin-hsien County did not come about overnight. They were the result of years of struggle and new forms of organization. The peasant family in the preceding story would be unable to conceive of the life that is characteristic of Lin-hsien today. What happened? Part of the answer to that question can be found in events that took place in a farming village not far from Lin-hsien County.

The year is 1947. The Japanese have recently been defeated in World War II by the Chinese and their allies after eight years of fighting on Chinese soil. But war continues in China. Now it is a civil war between the Communists, led by Mao Tse-tung, and the Nationalists (or Kuomintang), led by Chiang K'ai-shek, President of the Republic of China before the Communists gained control.

Stone Wall Village, where the story takes place, is in the Communist-held area of China. The Communists are promoting a campaign to redistribute land from the rich to the poor and to overthrow the old ruling class in the countryside. Stone Wall Village, like Lin-hsien, is in a very poor part of the country. In that respect it is not typical of all of China, but the events that took place there were similar to those that were to alter radically social relationships throughout China.

Jack Belden, *China Shakes the World* (New York: Monthly Review Press, 1972), pp. 174–88; abridged. Copyright © 1949 by Jack Belden. Reprinted by permission of Monthly Review Press.

As you read Part I of "Stone Wall Village Turns Over," think of the problems facing those who were promoting land reform. Why did revolution move slowly in China?⅋

THE LAND IN this region is rocky, bare of forest, and grudging in its fertility, so that the hard-pressed farmers have been forced to build terraces and cultivate the hill slopes nearly to the top of every peak. . . .

The common farmers, always hungry and always in debt, had a verse about their bitter lot, which ran like this:

> Harvest every year; but yearly—nothing.
> Borrow money yearly; yearly still in debt.
> Broken huts, small basins, crooked pots;
> Half an acre of land; five graves.

Politically, Stone Wall Village was in the hands of its village chief, a landlord named Wang Chang-ying. Although his personal characteristics are not germane to this story, it may be mentioned in passing that Landlord Wang was fifty years old, that he wore a small goatee and smoked a long-handled water pipe. In fair weather, it was said that he promenaded on the streets and beat any child who was unfortunate enough to bump into him. At the sight of him, many of the village poor would immediately run indoors.

Wang's possessions included sixty-five acres (no one else owned more than three) of irrigated land, the riverside mill, a large store of grain, one wife, one son, one daughter, one daughter-in-law, and a vengeful nature. . . .

Such was the condition of Stone Wall Village when the Chinese Revolution suddenly descended on it. There had been vague stories of this revolution in the village; there had been murmurings about the [Communist] 8th Route Army, about a thing called democracy, and about villages where there were no landlords and everyone had an equal amount of land. But the people had listened to these rumors with only half an ear; they were poor and fated to be poor; they did not want to fight anybody, they only wanted to be left alone.

Landlord Wang had also heard these rumors; he did not take them seriously either. But as a precaution, he used to tell the people: "Flesh cut from others won't stick to your own body." The people, however, did not need this warning: they had no intention of moving against Landlord Wang.

Nevertheless, the Revolution came to Stone Wall Village.

It did not come like a flash of swift lightning; for a revolution like everything else moves slowly in China. Nor did it announce itself like a clap of thunder, with the beat of drums, the sound of rifle fire, or hot slogans shouted on the country air.

To be more exact, five men brought the Revolution to Stone Wall Village. They were not soldiers, nor were they Communist Party members. One had been a schoolteacher, another a student, a third a waiter, a fourth a shop assistant, and the fifth a farmer. They were all members of the Ho-hsien County Salvation Association, and their job was to "overturn" Stone Wall Village.

"Overturn" is a term of the Chinese Revolution that came into being after the surrender of the Japanese. In Communist terminology, it means to turn over the social, political, and economic life of every village, to overturn feudalism and establish democracy, to overturn superstition and establish reason. The first step of the overturning movement is to "struggle" against the landlords and divide the land.

To do this sounds easy. You have the guns and the power, and you just tell the landlord to give a share of his land to the people. But it is never that easy. In Stone Wall Village, there was no army, there was no militia. The 8th Route Army was far to the south. Even the guerrillas had gone elsewhere. Landlord Wang was the power, and the people were afraid of him.

The leader of the Ho-hsien Salvation team was a thirty-one-year-old cadre [official], the son of a bankrupt rich farmer, named Chou Yu-chuan. When Chou and his fellow workers arrived in Stone Wall Village, they posted proclamations . . . announcing that every village had the right to elect its own

officials and that land rents and rates of interest should be reduced. Then they called a meeting to explain these proclamations, but the people listened only half-heartedly, kept their
mouths tightly shut, and went home without speaking further
to the cadres.

For several days, the cadres went individually among the
people, asking them about local conditions and their own lives,
but no one would talk. Whenever a cadre approached a group
of people, they would break apart and move away. One or two
men cornered alone admitted they were afraid of the landlord.

Under these conditions, the cadres could not carry on their
work, so they decided to seek out one of the poorer men in the
village and talk to him alone and in secret.

At this time, Chou and another cadre were living in a cave
next door to one occupied by a tenant farmer named Ma Chiu-
tze. Ma had bought his cave before the Japanese war with six
dollars earned by his wife spinning thread. Now his wife was
sick, and Ma often came to the cadres' cave and slept on the
same *k'ang* with them. During the night, the three men always
talked.

Ever since the Ch'ing dynasty [1644–1911], Ma revealed,
his family had been poor tenants, renting land and never having any of their own. Every year, he raised eight *piculs* [one
picul equals 133 pounds] of millet, and every year he had to
give four of these *piculs* to Landlord Wang. He could afford no
medicine for his wife, who he feared was dying. Two years
before, his father had died, and he had not been able to buy
the old man a coffin but had to wrap him in straw. Now he was
thirty-five and he was still poor and it looked as if he would
always be poor. "I guess I have a bad brain," he would say in
summing up the reasons for his poverty.

Then the cadres would ask: "Are you poor because you
have a bad brain or because your father left you no property?"

"I guess that's the reason; my father left me no property."

"Really, is that the reason?" asked the cadres. "Let us
make an account. You pay four *piculs* of grain every year to
the landlord. Your family has rented land for sixty years. That's

Chiang K'ai-shek in 1931, when, as leader of the Nationalist (Kuomin-tang) Army and government, he tried to destroy the Communist move-ment. He was finally defeated by the Communists in 1949. (From the collection of Edward C. Carter, at the University of Vermont.)

240 *piculs* of grain. If you had not given this to the landlord, you would be rich. The reason you are poor, then, is because you have been exploited by the landlord."

They would talk like this for hours, and Ma would finally acknowledge that he was exploited by the landlord. . . .

Ma agreed that the landlords had to be overthrown before there could be any happiness for the poor, but he was only half convinced of his own statements. There was yet a long distance between words and action, and the weight of two thousand years of tradition lay very heavily on Ma, as on most Chinese peasants.

For fifteen days, the cadres talked with Ma. In this period, they had twenty-three formal talks with him besides the numerous evening talks. They conversed with other farmers in the village, but Ma was the most "active" element. From this it can be seen it is not easy to stir a Chinese peasant.

Stone Wall Village Turns Over

≈§*Editor's Introduction:* The cadres who came to Stone Wall Village found that it is not easy to rouse a Chinese peasant to revolt. But slowly, together with their first convert, Ma, they convinced other poor peasants to join in the struggle against landlord Wang. As a warning to the would-be "overturners," the landlord had one of them, a man named Original Fortune Lee, murdered; thus the landlord drew the first blood.

As the account of events in Stone Wall Village continues, this incident has just taken place. Why did the peasants eventually rise up and overthrow Wang?§≈

AFTER THE MURDER of Original Fortune Lee, the people went about in terror and shut up again like clams. Even those who had attended the second meeting now said: "We haven't begun to struggle with the landlord, but one of us is gone already."

The cadres were very much surprised by the murder. They thought they had been too careless and had not placed enough belief in the peasants' fears. They also thought a hand grenade might be thrown at any time into their meeting cave. Their biggest fear, however, was that the peasants would give up the overturning movement altogether. Therefore, they decided to hold a memorial meeting in honor of Original Fortune Lee and by this meeting to mobilize the people. . . .

One hundred people of Stone Wall Village attended this

meeting, but Landlord Wang did not come. . . . The memorial meeting lasted four hours. After it was over, another meeting was called to decide how to continue "overturning." Only six farmers came to this meeting. No one said directly that he was afraid to attend, but they weakly gave the excuse: "I have a little work to do."

The six men, however, decided that because of the murder they would have to "settle" with Landlord Wang immediately.

At the end of five days, thirty farmers mobilized by the other six gathered in the cave for another meeting. Until nearly midnight, they told stories of how they had suffered at the landlord's hands.

Suddenly, someone said: "Maybe Wang will run away."

"Let's get him tonight," said several farmers at once.

After some discussion, they all trooped out of the cave and started a march on Landlord Wang's home. Among the thirty men, there was one rifle and three hand grenades.

The marching farmers separated into two groups. One climbed on top of the cliffs and worked along the cave roofs until they were over the courtyard. The others marched directly to the gate, knocked loudly, and commanded the landlord to open up.

Wang's wife answered the door and announced that her husband was not at home. Refusing to believe her, the peasants made a search and discovered a secret passage behind a cupboard. Descending through an underground tunnel, they found Wang cowering in a subterranean cave. They took him away and locked him up overnight. . . .

[The next] day, a mass meeting was called in a great square field south of the town, not far from the river. About eighty people came to complain against Wang, while the rest of the village watched—among them Wang's wife and daughter.

In the course of the morning and afternoon, the crowd accused the landlord of many crimes, including betraying resistance members to the Japanese, robbing them of grain, forcing them into labor gangs. At last, he was asked if he admitted the accusations.

"All these things I have done," he said, "but really it was not myself who did it, but the Japanese."

He could not have chosen worse words. Over the fields now sounded an angry roar, as of the sea, and the crowd broke into a wild fury. Everybody shouted at once, proclaiming against the landlord's words. Even the nonparticipating by-standers warmed to something akin to anger.

Then, above the tumult of the crowd, came a voice louder than the rest, shouting: "Hang him up!"

The chairman of the meeting and the cadres were disregarded. For all that the crowd noticed, they did not exist.

The crowd boiled around Wang, and somewhere a rope went swishing over a tree. Willing hands slung one end of the rope around Wang's waist. Other eager hands gave the rope a jerk. Wang rose suddenly and came to a halt in mid-air about three feet above the earth. And there he hung, his head down, his stomach horizontal and his legs stretched out—a perfect il-lustration of what the Chinese call a "duck's swimming form."

About his floating body, the crowd foamed, anger wrin-kling their foreheads and curses filling their mouths. Some bent down and spit in the landlord's eyes, and others howled into his ears.

As he rose from the ground, the landlord felt a terror that mounted higher as his position became more uncomfortable. Finally, he could bear it no longer and shouted: "Put me down. I know my wrongs. I admit everything."

The spite of the crowd, however, was not so easily as-suaged, and they only answered the landlord's pleas with shouts: "Pull him up! He's too low! Higher! Higher!"

After a while, the anger of the people abated and cooler heads counseled. "If we let him die now, we won't be able to settle accounts with him." Then they allowed him to come down for a rest.

At this point, the wife of Original Fortune Lee came up close to Wang and said in a plaintive voice: "Somebody killed my husband. Was it you?"

Wang's face, which had grown red from hanging in the air, slowly was drained of all color. "No, I did not do it," he said.

"Tell the truth," said the crowd. "You can admit everything to us and nothing will happen. But if you don't tell us the truth, we will hang you up again."

"No, it was not me."

These words were hardly out of his mouth before someone jerked on the rope and the landlord flew into the air again. This time the crowd let him hang for a long while. Unable to bear the pain, Wang finally said: "Let me down. I'll speak."

Then, between sobs and sighs, he told how he and his son had seized Original Fortune Lee as he was walking home from the meeting, tied his hands together, held his head under water until he was dead, and then had thrown him in the river, thinking he would float away.

A cry of rage went up as Wang finished speaking.

"You've already killed three of our men in the war," said Liu Kwang. "That could be excused. But now your own life can never repay us for the crimes you've done.". . .

A shout went up from the crowd as Landlord Wang was led to the field. Three guards marched him, pale and shaking, to a willow tree, where he was bound up. With his back against the tree, the landlord looked once at the crowd but quickly bent his head toward the ground again.

A slight shiver of apprehension went through the audience. They could not believe their enemy was helpless here before them. He was the lamb led to slaughter, but they could not quite believe they were going to kill him.

Ma Chiu-tze stepped before the crowd and called for attention.

"Now the time has come for our revenge," he announced in a trembling voice. "In what way shall we take revenge on this sinful landlord? We shall kill him."

A peasant strikes back. (From *Chinese Literature*, No. 3. Peking: Foreign Languages Press, 1972.)

As he said this, he turned around and slapped Wang sharply across the face.

The crack of palm against cheek rang like a pistol shot on

the morning air. A low animal moan broke from the crowd, and it leaped into action.

The landlord looked up as he heard the crowd rushing on him. Those nearest saw his lips move and heard him say: "Two words, two words, please."

The man closest shouted: "Don't let him speak!" and in the same breath swung his hoe, tearing the clothes from the bound man's chest and ripping open the lower portion of his body.

The landlord gave one chilling shriek and then bowed his head in resignation. The crowd was on him like beasts. Their faces had turned yellow and their eyes rolled. A big farmer swung his pig knife and plunged it directly into the landlord's heart. His body quivered—even the tree shook—then slumped, but still the farmer drew his knife in and out, again and again and yet once again.

Landlord Wang was quickly dead, but the rage of the crowd would not abate.

The field rang with the shouts of maddened people.

"It is not enough to kill him."

"We must put him in the open air."

"We must not allow him to be buried for three days."

But such convulsive passions do not last long. They burn themselves out. Slowly, the anger of the crowd cooled. The body of the landlord might rot in the open air, and it were better that his wife and daughter be allowed to get him.

That evening, as the sun was going down behind the mountain, the landlord's wife and daughter brought a mule cart slowly across the field to where their husband and father lay. They wept no tears but silently lifted the mutilated body into the cart and drove away.

Few saw them come and few saw them go. And no one said a word. For there was nothing left to say. The struggle against the landlord was ended.

Stone Wall Village had turned over.

"It's Terrible" or "It's Fine"

Editor's Introduction: Were the rage and violence of the peasants of Stone Wall Village necessary? Were they just? Your answer depends on your conception of necessity and justice. "Necessary" for what? "Just" by what standards?

People and nations through the ages have tried to justify violence; the bloodiest wars in history were fought in the name of justice, freedom, religion, even love.

The revolutionary must weigh the violence of overturning the old society against the violence of keeping it. In traditional China, for centuries there was at least one famine a year, on the average, in some part of the country. A famine in northwest China from 1928 to 1930 killed an estimated three to six million people. In 1943 alone, a famine in one province, Honan, killed three million. Incredibly, while some people were dying, others were hoarding grain. While some peasants sold their land and even their children for the price of a meal, unscrupulous landlords took advantage of the low prices to get rich.

Today the population of China is much bigger than ever before, but no one starves, because there was a violent revolution. Mao Tse-tung, the leader of that revolution, worked for years to overturn the landlord system. He wrote "It's Terrible" or "It's Fine" in 1927, in the very early stages of the land revolution. What does he say about revolutionary violence? Do you agree with his sentiments?

Mao Tse-tung, *Selected Works of Mao Tse-tung*, Vol. I (Peking: Foreign Languages Press, 1965), pp. 26–28; abridged.

Mao Tse-tung talking to peasants in the 1930s.

THE PEASANTS' REVOLT disturbed the gentry's sweet dreams. When the news from the countryside reached the cities, it caused immediate uproar among the gentry. Soon after my arrival in Changsha, I met all sorts of people and picked up a good deal of gossip. From the middle social strata upwards to the . . . right-wingers, there was not a single person who did not sum up the whole business in the phrase "It's terrible!" Under the impact of the views of the "It's terrible!" school then flooding the city, even quite revolutionary-minded people became downhearted as they pictured the events in the countryside in their mind's eye; and they were unable to deny the word "terrible." Even quite progressive people said, "Though terrible, it is inevitable in a revolution." In short, nobody could altogether deny the word "terrible."

But . . . the fact is that the great peasant masses have risen to fulfill their historic mission, and that the forces of rural democracy have risen to overthrow the forces of rural feudalism. . . . This is a marvelous feat never before achieved, not . . . in thousands of years. It's fine. It is not "terrible" at all. It is anything but "terrible." "It's terrible!" is obviously a theory for combating the rise of the peasants in the interests of the landlords; it is obviously a theory of the landlord class for preserving the old order of feudalism and obstructing the establishment of the new order of democracy, it is obviously a counterrevolutionary theory. No revolutionary comrade should echo this nonsense.

If your revolutionary viewpoint is firmly established and if you have been to the villages and looked around, you will undoubtedly feel thrilled as never before. Countless thousands of the enslaved—the peasants—are striking down the enemies who battened on their flesh. What the peasants are doing is absolutely right; what they are doing is fine! "It's fine!" is the theory of the peasants and of all other revolutionaries.

Every revolutionary comrade should know that the national revolution requires a great change in the countryside. The Revolution of 1911 [which overthrew the 2000-year-old imperial system and attempted to establish a republic] did not bring about this change; hence its failure. This change is now taking place, and it is an important factor for the completion of the revolution. Every revolutionary comrade must support it, or he will be taking the stand of counterrevolution.

The Question of "Going Too Far"

Then there is another section of people who say, "Yes, peasant associations are necessary, but they are going rather too far." This is the opinion of the middle-of-the-roaders. But what is the actual situation?

True, the peasants are in a sense "unruly" in the countryside. Supreme in authority, the peasant association allows the landlord no say and sweeps away his prestige. This amounts to striking the landlord down to the dust and keeping him there. The peasants threaten, "We will put you in the other register!" They fine the local tyrants and evil gentry, they demand contributions from them, and they smash their sedan-chairs. People swarm into the houses of local tyrants and evil gentry who are against the peasant association, slaughter their pigs, and consume their grain. They even loll for a minute or two on the ivory-inlaid beds belonging to the young ladies in these households. . . . At the silghtest provocation, they make arrests, crown the arrested with tall paper hats, and parade them through the villages, saying, "You dirty landlords, now you know who we are!" Doing whatever they like and turning everything upside down, they have created a kind of terror in the countryside. This is what some people call "going too far," or "exceeding the proper limits in righting a wrong," or "really too much."

Such talk may seem plausible, but in fact it is wrong. First, the local tyrants, evil gentry, and lawless landlords have themselves driven the peasants to this. For ages they have used their power to tyrannize the peasants and trample them underfoot; that is why the peasants have reacted so strongly. The most violent revolts and the most serious disorders have invariably occurred in places where the local tyrants, evil gentry, and lawless landlords perpetrated the worst outrages.

The peasants are clear-sighted. Who is bad and who is not, who is the worst and who is not quite so vicious, who deserves severe punishment and who deserves to be let off lightly—the peasants keep clear accounts, and very seldom has the punishment exceeded the crime.

Second, a revolution is not a dinner party, or writing an essay, or painting a picture, or doing embroidery; it cannot be so refined, so leisurely and gentle, so temperate, kind, courteous, restrained, and magnanimous. A revolution is an insurrection, an act of violence by which one class overthrows another. A rural revolution is a revolution by which the peasantry overthrows the power of the feudal landlord class. Without using the greatest force, the peasants cannot possibly overthrow the deep-rooted authority of the landlords, which has lasted for thousands of years. The rural areas need a mighty revolutionary upsurge, for it alone can rouse the people in their millions to become a powerful force.

ℛ𝒶· The Long March

✑§*Editor's Introduction:* Twenty-two years elapsed between the time Mao wrote " 'It's Terrible' or 'It's Fine' " and the Communist conquest of China in 1949. Conditions were right for the Communist movement, but the road to power was not without its twists, turns, and detours.

The Communist Party of China was founded in 1921. It grew slowly in the 1920's, but it did not develop large-scale mass support until the early 1930's, when Mao Tse-tung and General Chu Te established a base in a rural area in south-central China and began to redistribute land.

The Nationalist government, which supported the landlords, turned all its might against the Communists and, after five "extermination campaigns," managed to drive them from their base area in 1934. Those Communists who escaped the Nationalist attack embarked on a 6,000-mile trek, which is now called "the Long March."

The Long March was the turning point in the Chinese Communist movement. Against enormous odds, the Communists marched and fought their way to a safe area in northwest China. In 368 days, an army of tens of thousands with all its equipment covered an average of almost twenty-four miles per day when on the move. They crossed eighteen mountain ranges, five of them perennially snow-capped, and sixty-two rivers. All the while, they fought an average of a skirmish a day and spent fifteen whole days fighting major battles.

Yang Chengwu, "Lightening Attack on the Luting Bridge," in Deirdre and Neale Hunter, *We the Chinese, Voices from China* (New York: Praeger, 1971), pp. 34–41; abridged.

In every area they passed through, they publicized their movement in mass meetings and theatrical performances. More important, they redistributed the land and other property of the landlords to the poor peasants, leaving in their wake thousands of armed peasants and cadres to train guerrilla forces.

The Communists emerged from the Long March with heavy losses, but confident that they had passed the severest of tests and that nothing could prevent their ultimate victory. Today the Long March is celebrated in song and story as the great epic of the Communists' rise to power. It represents a triumph of human will and endurance in overcoming the most difficult obstacles.

Numerous accounts of the March have been collected and widely publicized in China. In the one that follows, a Communist regimental commander who participated in the action recalls the crucial battle for the Lu-ting Bridge, which crosses the swift Ta-tu River. Had the Communists not captured the bridge, they almost surely would have been trapped and destroyed by Chiang K'ai-shek's troops. As the narrative begins, the Communist troops on one side of the Ta-tu River are racing some of Chiang K'ai-shek's troops (the enemy in the story) on the other. Each army is trying to reach the Lu-ting Bridge first.

What lessons does this chapter in the great epic of the Long March hold for Chinese who read it today?

SUDDENLY A FEW flickering lights appeared on the opposite side of the river. The next moment, they grew into a long string of torches. The enemy troops were making a forced march by torchlight! I immediately conferred with our regimental commander, our chief of staff, and our Party secretary. We decided that we, too, would carry torches. Should the enemy signal across the river and ask us to identify ourselves, we would pretend we were the three enemy battalions we had already defeated. We directed our bugler to be prepared to sound the calls used by the enemy. Since the enemy troops were all [from the province of Szechuan], we picked some Szechuan men from our own ranks and from the prisoners to shout back replies to any questions.

We bought reeds from the folks in the hamlet, made torches, and issued one to each man, with instructions that they were not to be wasted.

Our aim was to cover at least three miles per hour. I had a leg wound that was causing me some inconvenience, and the comrades, especially the regimental commander, urged me to continue on horseback. But I decided it was my duty as an officer to set an example. Instead of riding, I issued a challenge, "We will all march together, comrades. Let's see who walks the fastest. Let's see who gets to the Lu-ting Bridge first!"

Taking up the challenge, the men held their torches high and pressed forward.

Torchlight crimsoned the waters of the Ta-tu. Our lights and those of the enemy writhed along the river banks like two fiery dragons.

The sharp notes of an enemy bugle rang out, followed by the cry, "Which unit are you?" Our bugler blew the necessary call, and our Szechuan men shouted a reply. The enemy was fooled. They never suspected that the gallant Red Army they hoped to wipe out was marching parallel with them.

They stayed with us for almost ten miles. Around midnight, the rain grew heavier, and the torches on the opposite bank disappeared. We guessed they had found the going too hard and encamped. The news spread quickly through the regiment, causing many comments among the men: "This is our chance! March on! Faster!" In single file, we pushed on for all we were worth.

The rain pelted down mercilessly and the mountain gullies turned into rushing torrents. The twisting path became as slippery as oil, so that our walking staffs were of little use. We could not march; we slipped and slithered, scrambled and crawled along. And when we came to an even stretch, the weary men would doze off as they walked. A soldier would come to a halt and the comrade behind would push him and yell, "Keep going! Keep going!" The man would awaken and hurry to catch up. Finally the men took off their puttees [leg wrappings] and tied themselves together in a long chain.

In this way we kept up the forced march all night and reached our destination on time. In twenty-four hours, in addition to fighting and repairing wrecked bridges, we had covered eighty miles. This was truly an exploit of winged feet.

We first captured the west bank and the western approaches to the Lu-ting Bridge. Having occupied several buildings and a Catholic church, our men prepared for the coming battle. Regimental Commander Wang and I went out with the battalion and company officers to study the situation. We were taken aback by the difficulties to be overcome. The river's reddish waters cascaded down the mountain gorges of the upper reaches and pounded against ugly boulders in midstream, tossing white foam high into the air. The roar of the rushing water was deafening. Fording or crossing in boats was out of the question.

We examined the bridge. It was made of iron chains, thirteen in number, each link as thick as a rice bowl. Two chains on each side served as hand-railings; the other nine formed a catwalk. Planks had originally been laid across these, but they had been taken by the enemy, leaving only the black chains hanging in mid-air.

At the head of the bridge, on a stone slab, two lines from a poem were inscribed:

Towering mountains flank the Lu-ting Bridge,
Their summits rise a hundred miles into the clouds.

The city of Lu-ting lay directly beyond the eastern end of the bridge. It was built half along the shore and half on the mountain slope and was surrounded by a wall over twenty feet high. The west gate of this wall was just past the end of the bridge. The city was garrisoned by two enemy regiments, and strong fortifications had been built along the mountainside. Machine-gun emplacements close to the bridge kept us under continual fire, and mortar shells rained down on us.

The enemy was confident that this position was impregnable. "Let's see you fly across!" they yelled. "We'll give up our arms if you can do it!"

Our soldiers shouted back: "We don't want your arms. We want your bridge!"

Back from our reconnaissance, we first positioned a battalion to cover the path on the other side of the river. That was the only way enemy reinforcements could come. Then we went round our companies to begin the battle rallies. Morale was high. Each company submitted a list of volunteers for an assault party, and each wanted to be given the honor of taking the bridge. . . .

The attack began at four o'clock in the afternoon. The regimental commander and I directed it from the west end of the bridge. The buglers gathered together to sound the charge, and we opened up with every weapon we had. The sound of the bugles, the firing, and the shouts of the men reverberated through the valley.

Then the twenty-two heroes, led by Commander Liao, climbed out cross the swaying chains in the teeth of intense enemy fire. Each man carried a tommy gun, a broadsword, and twelve hand grenades. Behind them came the officers and men of the Third Company, each carrying a heavy plank as well as full battle gear. They fought and laid planks at the same time.

Just as the assault force reached the eastern bridgehead, huge flames sprang into the sky outside the city gate. The enemy was trying to throw a wall of fire across our path. The blaze licked fiercely around the end of the bridge.

The outcome of the attack was hanging by a hair. The assault squad hesitated for a few seconds, then plunged boldly into the flames. Commander Liao's cap caught fire, but he threw it away and fought on. The others also dashed through the flames and smashed their way into the city. In the street fighting that followed, the enemy brought their full weight to bear against our gallant force. Our men fought until all their ammunition was spent. There was a critical pause as the Third Company came charging to their rescue. Then Regimental Commander Wang and I sped across the bridge with our reinforcements and entered the city.

In two hours, we had destroyed over half of the enemy's

Storming the Lu-ting Bridge over the Ta-tu River. Oil painting.

two regiments, and the remainder broke ranks and scattered. By dusk we had completely occupied the city of Lu-ting and were in control of the bridge. . . .

General Liu examined every detail of the iron chains as if he were trying to memorize the entire bridge. On the way back, he stopped in the middle and leaned over the side chains to look down on the turbulent waters of the Ta-tu below. Tapping his foot on the boards, he murmured, "We've spent plenty of blood and energy to get you, Lu-ting Bridge, but we've got you!"

The following day, Commander Lin Piao marched up with our main force. . . . Then Chairman Mao arrived, and thousands of our troops marched across the Lu-ting Bridge. We had conquered the seething barrier of the Ta-tu River.

Editor's Postscript: The Communists arrived in northwest China after the Long March with only about 30,000 men. They occupied an area that was easy to defend but sparsely populated, and noted for its poverty. Fewer than one million people lived in the Communist area in early 1937. But in 1949, only twelve years later, the Communists controlled the whole China mainland. Only Taiwan (Formosa) and a few other islands remained in the hands of Chiang K'ai-shek and the former government of China.

The success of the Communists can be explained by a number of factors. The war with Japan from 1937 to 1945 disrupted the country. And during the war, Chiang K'ai-shek's government became corrupt and inefficient. But the main reason for the Communist victory is summarized in a few words from a study made by the U.S. War Department (now called the Department of Defense) in 1945:

> Practically all impartial observers emphasized that the Chinese Communists comprise the most efficient, politically well-organized, disciplined, and constructive group in China today. This opinion is well supported by facts. It is largely because of their political and military skill, superior organization, and progressive attitude, which has won for them a popular support no other party or group in China can equal, that they have been expanding their influence throughout the past seven years.*

* Lyman P. Van Slyke, ed., *The Chinese Communist Movement, A Report of the U.S. War Department,* July, 1945 (Stanford: Stanford University Press, 1968), pp. 7–8.

Maoist Ethics—
The "Three Constantly Read Articles"

◄§ *Editor's Introduction:* The "progressive attitude" attributed to the Communists by the U.S. War Department study in 1945 is illustrated in "The Three Constantly Read Articles," all of which were written by Mao Tse-tung in the 1930s and 1940s. The Communists were convinced that a genuine and lasting revolution would depend not only on institutional change, such as land reform, but also on a change in the way people think.

Like their Confucian predecessors, the Communists are very concerned with thought, for they believe that ideas and action are closely related. "Correct" ideas will lead to "correct" actions and vice versa. In the past, as in the present, there has been a single orthodoxy in China with little tolerance for deviation.

The three short pieces in this chapter were chosen by Mao Tse-tung from the hundreds of articles he had written as most representative of the values which he hoped would provide the guidelines for the new China. Originally addressed to members of the Communist Party, they later became essential reading for a nation. What are the values expressed? ε◄

Mao Tse-tung, *Five Articles by Chairman Mao Tse-tung* (Peking: Foreign Languages Press, 1967), pp. 1-19; abridged.

Serve the People

September 8, 1944

IF WE HAVE shortcomings, we are not afraid to have them pointed out and criticized, because we serve the people. Anyone, no matter who, may point out our shortcomings. If he is right, we will correct them. If what he proposes will benefit the people, we will act upon it. . . .

If, in the interests of the people, we persist in doing what is right and correct what is wrong, our ranks will surely thrive.

We hail from all corners of the country and have joined together for a common revolutionary objective. And we need the vast majority of the people with us on the road to this objective. Today, we already lead base areas with a population of 91 million, but this is not enough; to liberate the whole nation more are needed. In times of difficulty we must not lose sight of our achievements, must see the bright future and must pluck up our courage. The Chinese people are suffering; it is our duty to save them and we must exert ourselves in struggle. Wherever there is struggle there is sacrifice, and death is a common occurrence.

But we have the interests of the people and the sufferings of the great majority at heart, and when we die for the people it is a worthy death. Nevertheless, we should do our best to avoid unnecessary sacrifices. Our cadres must show concern for every soldier, and all people in the revolutionary ranks must care for each other, must love and help each other. . . .

In Memory of Norman Bethune

December 21, 1939

Comrade Norman Bethune, a member of the Communist Party of Canada, was around fifty when he was sent by the Communist parties of Canada and the United States to China; he made light of traveling thousands of miles to help us in our War of Resistance against Japan. He arrived in Yenan in the spring of last year, went to work in the Wutai Mountains, and to our great sorrow died a martyr at his post.

What kind of spirit is this that makes a foreigner selflessly adopt the cause of the Chinese people's liberation as his own? It is the spirit of internationalism, the spirit of communism, from which every Chinese Communist must learn. . . .

Comrade Bethune's spirit, his utter devotion to others without any thought of self, was shown in his boundless sense of responsibility in his work and his boundless warmhearted-ness toward all comrades and the people. Every Communist must learn from him. There are not a few people who are irre-sponsible in their work, preferring the light to the heavy, shov-ing the heavy loads on to others and choosing the easy ones for themselves. At every turn they think of themselves before oth-ers. When they make some small contribution, they swell with pride and brag about it for fear that others will not know. They feel no warmth toward comrades and the people but are cold, indifferent, and apathetic. In fact such people are not Commu-nists, or at least cannot be counted as true Communists. No one who returned from the front failed to express admiration for Bethune whenever his name was mentioned, and none re-mained unmoved by his spirit. . . . Every Communist must learn this true communist spirit from Comrade Bethune.

Comrade Bethune was a doctor, the art of healing was his profession, and he was constantly perfecting his skill, which stood very high in the 8th Route Army's medical service. His example is an excellent lesson for those people who wish to change their work the moment they see something different, and for those who despise technical work as of no consequence or as promising no future.

Comrade Bethune and I met only once. Afterward he wrote me many letters. But I was busy, and I wrote him only one letter and do not even know if he ever received it. I am deeply grieved over his death. Now we are all commemorating him, which shows how profoundly his spirit inspires everyone. We must all learn the spirit of absolute selflessness from him. With this spirit everyone can be very useful to the people. A man's ability may be great or small, but if he has this spirit, he is already noble-minded and pure, a man of moral integrity and above vulgar interests, a man who is of value to the people.

The Foolish Old Man Who Removed the Mountains

June 11, 1945

. . . There is an ancient Chinese fable called "The Foolish Old Man Who Removed the Mountains." It tells of an old man who lived in northern China long, long ago and was known as the Foolish Old Man of North Mountain.

Moving   the   mountains.

His house faced south, and beyond his doorway stood the two great peaks, Tai-hang and Wang-wu, obstructing the way. With great determination, he led his sons in digging up these mountains hoe in hand. Another graybeard, known as the Wise Old Man, saw them and said derisively, "How silly of you to do this! It is quite impossible for you few to dig up these two huge mountains." The Foolish Old Man replied, "When I die, my sons will carry on; when they die, there will be my grand-sons, and then their sons and grandsons, and so on to infinity. High as they are, the mountains cannot grow any higher and with every bit we dig, they will be that much lower. Why can't we clear them away?"

Having refuted the Wise Old Man's wrong view, he went on digging every day, unshaken in his conviction. God was moved by this, and he sent down two angels, who carried the mountains away on their backs.

Today, two big mountains lie like a dead weight on the Chinese people. One is imperialism, the other is feudalism. The Chinese Communist Party has long made up its mind to dig them up. We must persevere and work unceasingly, and we, too, will touch God's heart. Our God is none other than the masses of the Chinese people. If they stand up and dig to-gether with us, why can't these two mountains be cleared away? . . .

Studying the "Three Constantly Read Articles." (From *Jen-min hua-pao*, 1970, No. 12, p. 53.)

The Traditional Family Ethic

≈§ Editor's Introduction: The values expressed by Mao in the "Three Constantly Read Articles" are both a product of, and a departure from, traditional Chinese ethics. The Chinese have always rejected individualism, so valued in the West, considering it synonymous with selfishness.

The selfless, collective ethic espoused by Mao is also found in the family ethic of traditional China. Mao simply extended it to a broader social context, but in so doing he signaled a monumental change.

For thousands of years the family was the basic social unit in China. Honor and obedience to one's parents and older relatives was the cardinal virtue. The collective family was the principal unit for welfare and social security. The government did little or nothing to provide health insurance or old age pensions. That was left to families. It was an unforgivable breach of ethics to neglect one's parents in their retirement.

To strengthen the family unit, the Chinese often formed clans composed of several generations and many branches of the male line of a family. Large clans included hundreds of members. A certain amount of land would be owned communally and used to support an ancestral temple, a school, a welfare fund, commercial operations, and so on. Clan rules defined proper behavior for all members. To violate those rules and be expelled from the clan was the worst thing that could happen to one of its members, for an expelled person would become isolated and trusted by no one.

Aside from its obligation to obey the laws of the land, the family owed little allegiance to anyone. Rich families felt but slight obligation to aid the poor, and indeed felt justified in pressing their economic and political advantages over them.

The collective ethic of the Communists was an attempt to expand the unit of social concern from the family to the whole society. The implications of that change are suggested in the following selection written in 1935 by Lin Yu-tang, a man in love with traditional Chinese culture but also capable of seeing its weaknesses. Compare his description of the old family ethic with the values espoused by Mao Tse-tung. �

THE CHINESE ARE . . . family-minded, not social-minded, and the family mind is only a form of magnified selfishness. It is curious that the word "society" does not exist as an idea in Chinese thought. . . . "Public spirit" is a new term, so is "civic consciousness," and so is "social service." There are no such commodities in China. . . .

To a Chinese, social work always looks like meddling with other people's business. A man enthusiastic for social reform or in fact for any kind of public work always looks a little bit ridiculous. We discount his sincerity. We cannot understand him. What does he mean by going out of his way to do all this work? Is he courting publicity? Why is he not loyal to his family, and why does he not get official promotion and help his family first? We decide he is young, or else he is a deviation from the normal human type.

There were always such deviations from type . . . but they were invariably of the bandit or vagabond class, unmarried, . . . willing to jump into the water to save an unknown drowning child. (Married men in China do not do that.) Or else they were married men who died penniless and made their wives and children suffer. . . .

The best modern educated Chinese still cannot understand why Western women should organize a "Society for the Prevention of Cruelty to Animals." Why bother about the dogs,

Lin Yu-t'ang, *My Country and My People* (New York: John Day, 1935), pp. 172-83; abridged. Copyright © 1935 by Lin Yu-t'ang.

(Courtesy Jean Elliott Johnson.)

why do they not stay at home and nurse their babies? We decide that these women have no children and therefore have
nothing better to do, which is probably often true. The conflict
is between the family mind and the social mind. If one
scratches deep enough, one always finds the family mind at
work.

For the family system is the root of Chinese society, from
which all Chinese social characteristics derive. . . . It touches
us even in very personal ways. It takes the right of contracting
marriage from our hands and gives it to our parents; it makes us
marry, not wives, but "daughters-in-law," and it makes our
wives give birth, not to children, but to "grandchildren." It
multiplies the obligations of the bride a hundredfold. It makes
it rude for a young couple to close the door of their room in
the family house in the daytime, and makes privacy an unknown word in China. . . .

The Doctrine of Social Status, as Confucianism has been
popularly called, is the social philosophy behind the family

system. It is the doctrine that makes for social order in China. It is the principle of social structure and social control at the same time. . . .

In theory at least, Confucius did not mean family consciousness to degenerate into a form of magnified selfishness at the cost of social integrity. . . . He meant the moral training in the family as the basis for general moral training, and he planned that from the general moral training a society should emerge which would live happily and harmoniously together. Only in this sense can one understand the tremendous emphasis placed on "filial piety" [respect for parents], which is regarded as the "first of all virtues.". . .

Confucius said:

The reason why the gentleman teaches filial piety is not because it is to be seen in the home and everyday life. He teaches filial piety in order that man may respect all those who are fathers in the world. He teaches brotherliness in the younger brother, in order that man may respect all those who are elder brothers in the world. He teaches the duty of the subject, in order that man may respect all who are rulers in the world.

Again, Confucius said:

Those who love their parents dare not show hatred to others. Those who respect their parents dare not show rudeness to others. . . .

Every family in China is really a communistic unit, with the principle of "do what you can and take what you need" guiding its functions. Mutual helpfulness is developed to a very high degree, encouraged by a sense of moral obligation and family honor. Sometimes a brother will cross the sea thousands of miles away to redeem the honor of a bankrupt brother. A well-placed and comparatively successful man generally contributes the greater, if not the entire, share of the expenses of the whole household, and it is common practice, worthy of no special merit, for a man to send his nephews to school. A successful man, if he is an official, always gives the best jobs

Several generations under one roof—a traditional Chinese ideal.
(From Robert Goldston, *The Rise of Red China*, Indianapolis:
Bobbs Merrill, 1967.)

to his relatives, and if there are not ready jobs, he can create
sinecure ones. Thus sinecurism and nepotism developed, which,
coupled with economic pressure, became an irresistible force,
undermining . . . any political reform movement. The force
is so great that repeated efforts at reform, with the best of intentions, have proved unsuccessful.

To look at it kindly, nepotism is no worse than favoritism
of other sorts. An official does not place only his nephews in
the office, but he also has to place the nephews of other high
officials . . . , who write him letters of recommendation. Where
is he going to place them except in sinecure posts and "ad-
visorships"? . . .

It is quite natural that charity should begin at home. For
the family system must be taken as the Chinese traditional
system of insurance against unemployment. Every family takes

care of its own unemployed, and . . . its next best work is to find employment for them. It is better than charity because it teaches in the less lucky members a sense of independence, and the members so helped in turn help other members of the family. Besides, the minister who robs the nation to feed the family, either for the present or for the next three or four generations, by amassing half a million to ten million or more dollars, is only trying to glorify his ancestors and be a "good" man of the family. . . .

Certain social characteristics arise from the family system, apart from nepotism and official corruption. They may be summed up as the lack of social discipline. It defeats any form of social organization, as it defeats the civil-service system through nepotism. It makes a man "sweep the snow in front of his door, and not bother about the frost on his neighbor's roof." This is not so bad. What is worse is that it makes a man throw his refuse outside his neighbor's door. . . .

Religion in Traditional China

The gods? Worship them by all means. But if you had only Lord Kuan and the Goddess of Mercy and no peasant association, could you have overthrown the local tyrants and evil gentry? The gods and goddesses are indeed miserable objects. You have worshipped them for centuries, and they have not overthrown a single one of the local tyrants or evil gentry for you! Now you want to have your rent reduced. Let me ask how will you go about it. Will you believe in the gods or in the peasant associations?

MAO TSE-TUNG, 1927

✍ Editor's Introduction: Changing the way people think requires more than a transformation of secular values. It also means changing religious ideas and institutions.

The Communists are atheists; they do not believe in any god or supernatural force. Rather, they assert that only living beings have ideas, and that those ideas did not exist before life on earth. In other words, they do not believe in a Grand Idea or master plan of God that existed before material reality and shaped it. Furthermore, they assert that there are no gods to help or to punish human beings. They believe that people make their own history in accordance with material reality. History and environment are what influence ideas and actions.

Francis Hsu, *Americans and Chinese* (New York: Doubleday Natural History Press, 1972), pp. 226—42; abridged.

Karl Marx, after studying history, concluded that human society is moving toward Communism—that is, toward a system in which everyone is equal and no person or group exploits another. The future can be foreseen to some extent, Marx felt, because of trends apparent in historical development so far, not because of a divine plan.

Mao Tse-tung, among all the followers of Marx, has particularly stressed that Communism is not predetermined. There is no mysterious force that makes the realization of Communism certain. And while firmly believing that Communist egalitarianism is good and worth struggling to achieve, he constantly reiterates that only humans can bring it about. To do so, they must get rid of all their superstitions and traditional ideas about gods and fate.

To understand what this task entails in the Chinese context, we must put aside for the moment our Western notions about religion. We must begin with an awareness that the Chinese were not Christians or Jews. Hard as the Christian missionaries tried before the Communists came to power, they never converted more than half of 1 per cent of the population to Christianity. Nor were all Chinese Buddhists, as so many Westerners tend to believe. Buddhism had its day in China as the major religion of the country, but the great age of Buddhism ended by about 900 A.D. In the last Chinese dynasty (1644-1912), Buddhism was actually outlawed but was unofficially tolerated as long as it did not interfere with affairs of state.

The following selection, written by Francis Hsu, a Chinese anthropologist now teaching in the United States, describes the place of Buddhism and other religious beliefs in traditional Chinese society. How do traditional Chinese religious beliefs compare to those in Western society? How would they hinder revolutionary change?

IT IS COMPLETELY inaccurate to describe the Chinese . . . as Buddhists, Taoists, Confucianists, or ancestor-worshippers in the same sense that we classify Americans as Jews, Protestants, or Catholics . . . . [A] Chinese may go to a Buddhist monastery to pray for a male heir, but he may proceed from there to a Taoist shrine where he beseeches a god to cure him of malaria. Ask any number of Chinese what their religion is and the answer of the majority will be that they have no particular religion, or that, since all religions benefit man in one way or another, they are all equally good. Most Chinese temples . . .

are dedicated to the worship of many gods, and few family shrines are a sanctuary for only a single deity. There are many Chinese temples built expressly to house together Confucius, Buddha, and Lao Tze, the founder of Taoism. In prayer meetings staged by several southwestern Chinese communities during World War II, I saw included at many an altar the images of not only the numerous Chinese deities but also of Jesus Christ and Mohammed. . . . For the Chinese way in religion is to be more and more inclusive so that my god, your god, his god, and all gods, whether you or I know anything about them or not, must be equally honored or at least not be the objects of either my contempt or of yours. . . .

In every Chinese village we find a variety of temples all dedicated to the worship of many different gods. A typical village temple usually houses the Goddess of Mercy, who answers all kinds of prayers; the God of Wealth, who is indispensable to all businessmen; the Dragon God, who brings rain in times of drought; and the Earth God . . . , who is the local emissary of the other world. The inventory of gods in city temples is much larger. There are temples housing the God of Literature; Confucius and his seventy-two famous disciples; the God of Agriculture; the God of Medicine; the Goddess of Measles, Eyes, and other ailments or bodily parts; Ch'eng Huang, or God of the District, flanked by courts of the ten judges . . . and the gods who are said to be founders and patron deities of various crafts. . . . No one knows how many gods there are in China. There seems to be no limit to them, and most of them are unrelated to each other. . . .

I do not know of a single city or town in mainland China before 1949, or in Taiwan today, that is without diviners or geomancy readers, physiognomists, phrenologists, mediums, and all kinds of fortunetellers. For a fee, these persons offer to foretell the length of a person's life and his business prospects, or to determine the marriageability of a boy and girl, or to decide on the ritual suitability of a new house site or graveyard. They will often undertake to arrange a meeting or communication with the gods or with one's ancestors. There is literally no question they do not attempt to answer and almost no matter relating to the gods that they refuse to interpret. It is safe to say that no individual of prominence in traditional China failed to have his fate told, not once, but many times, by different professional fortunetellers. . . .

After death, the soul of every Chinese is subject, according to its deserts, to reward, punishment, or both. The courts of the ten judges, each of which successively reviews the merits and demerits of every newly departed soul, are well known among the Chinese for the tortures they may inflict. A soul may be sawed in half, restored, and then boiled in oil, next ground to a mush, then slowly drowned in a river of blood, after which its eyes are poked out and its tongue cut off, and so on ad nauseam. After all of these exasperating experiences,

Hired mourners in a traditional funeral procession. (Photo by Peter J. Seybolt.)

the soul may yet be banished to more suffering in one or all of the numerous hells. Some Chinese sources indicate that there are eighteen hells, one situated on top of the other, while other sources insist that there are many more.

A meritorious person's soul is treated very differently. Immediately after its departure from the body, it is met at the threshold of the world of spirits by a special reception party, playing music and bearing food that has been dispatched by one of the judges. The newcomer progresses from court to court, residing in guest houses at each stopping place. On these occasions he is entertained lavishly for long periods of time and has various honors conferred on him. He may then be offered an appointment as a local god upon earth or as a higher official in the court of the Supreme Ruler. If especially deserving, he may ultimately be entitled to a place of eternal happiness in the Western Paradise. . . .

ANCESTOR WORSHIP

I know of no Chinese, save the relatively few Christians and Mohammedans, who do not adhere to [the cult of ancestor worship.] It is literally the universal religion of China. . . .

Ancestor worship is an active ingredient in every aspect of Chinese society, from the family to the government, from local business to the national economy.

The Chinese have at least three basic assumptions about ancestor worship. First, all living persons owe their fortunes or misfortunes to their ancestors. A man may be a beggar because of his laziness, and this fact may be well known to everyone in the community; but had his ancestors accumulated enough good deeds while they were alive, they probably never would have had such a lazy descendant. A great official may attain prominence by excellence of scholarship and strength of character, and everyone who knows him may testify to these virtues. But his very achievement is evidence of his ancestors' high moral worth. . . .

The second assumption of ancestor worship is that all departed ancestors, like other gods and spirits, have needs that are not different from those of the living. To prevent one's ancestors from degenerating into spiritual vagabonds, it is the duty of every man to provide for his departed ancestors just as faithfully as he provides for his parents while they are alive. Accordingly, the dead, to the limit of the male descendant's financial ability, must be offered food and life-sized paper models of clothing, furniture, sedan chairs, horses, donkeys, cows, and servants, so that the departed may set up house in the other world . . .

This concept explains why a Chinese man or woman who dies without male heirs is an object of public pity. For that person is doomed to an existence as spirit tramps, depending entirely upon handouts from charitable families or consuming the leftovers of better situated spirits. . . .

The third assumption is that the departed ancestors continue, as in life, to assist their relatives in this world, just as their living descendants can also lend a hand to them. That is, a person's present lot may be improved by the spiritual efforts of departed ancestors, and the spiritual welfare or misery of a departed ancestor may likewise be enhanced or mitigated by the worldly actions of living descendants. . . .

[In short, the] Chinese maintain a positive and close relationship with their departed ancestors just as they do with their living kinsmen, while their attitude toward the other gods is neutral and distant, reflecting their attitudes toward the emperor and his officials. . . .

Religion in China Today

e3Editor's Introduction: When the Communists came to power in 1949, they did not outlaw religion. Much as they disliked it, they realized that beliefs that had been held for hundreds or thousands of years could not be eliminated by a law or by force. The following article from a Chinese newspaper explains the Communists' approach to the problem.

What, specifically, did the Communists find objectionable about traditional religious and superstitious practices in China? What was their policy for dealing with them?3∞

AMONG THE PEOPLE of our country, those who really believe in any religion and are followers of any religion are numerically in the minority. But, among the peasants especially, those who believe in the existence of spirits and gods, in fate, and in such superstition as fortunetelling are still quite numerous. In view of this, we must be good not only at struggling against religious superstitions but also at struggling against all other kinds of ordinary superstitious activities. . . .

In the old society a great number of people lived by swindling money and goods from the laboring people with these superstitious activities and formed specialized occupations of them. They included, for instance, physiognomists, geomancers, fortune-tellers, priestesses, godly men, and priests.

"On the Question of Religion and Superstition," *Jen-min jih-pao* (People's Daily), Peking, August 8, 1963.

68

Apart from serving the interests of the exploiting class, these themselves constituted a part of the exploiting classes.

After the nationwide liberation, educated and transformed by the Party and the People's Government, some of these people have really changed their occupations and trades and become part of the laboring people. But there are also many who have not yet been thoroughly transformed. When an opportunity presents itself, they will . . . resume their old trades and take advantage of the remnant superstitious thoughts of the masses of the people, mainly the peasants, continuing

Six per cent of the Chinese population belong to national minority groups. Pictured is a Kazakh folk musician. He too is Chinese. (From China Reconstructs, *July, 1973.)*

their activities of swindling the masses of their money and goods and continuing to exploit the people. . . .

Among the people of our country, especially the peasants, these ideas are still quite widespread. To varying extents, they still believe that after a man has died, he becomes a ghost. So the thought that ghosts are terrible is still comparatively widespread. Because of this thought, when a man has died, they will burn imitation money, paper clothes, paper horses, paper houses, etc., for him, so that his soul may use them in another world—the underworld. On the Chinese New Year's Day and on festive occasions, as well as on death anniversaries, they still go to cemeteries to offer sacrifices. Some, when they fall sick, will "send off the ghosts," or go to a temple to "make vows." And so forth. These superstitious activities are spontaneous and as a rule have no direct connection with those engaging in superstitious trades. We must strictly distinguish between the people's theist ideas and spontaneous superstitious activities, and the activities of those engaging in superstitious trades who swindle money and goods from the people through superstition. . . .

Our purpose in conducting education in atheism is to persuade people to give up their theism and religious superstitions and gradually become atheists. So we must take the attitude of "honest advice and proper guidance." If we hurt their feelings, they will then not listen to us however sound our reasoning may be. To avoid hurting the feelings of others, we must adhere to the principle of voluntariness. It is up to a man himself to choose between giving up and not giving up his theist ideas and religious superstitions and between accepting and not accepting the atheist thought. Nobody else may apply pressure to force him. Comrade Mao Tse-tung pointed out clearly, "We may not use administrative orders in eliminating religion or force people not to believe in religion. We may not force people . . . to believe in Marxism. All problems of an ideological nature can be solved only by means of discussion, criticism, and persuasive education. No attempt may be made to solve them by means of coercion and suppression. . . .

In other words, in conducting propaganda on atheism or opposing religious superstitions, we must absolutely not interfere with others' worship or tamper with the proper religious activities of the believers. On the other hand, the believers and theists, for their part, must not interfere with our conducting education in atheism or our opposing religious superstitions. Only this is the correct attitude.

Maoism as Religion

❧Editor's Introduction: The Communists have not always adhered to the principle of noninterference with religious activities. Many places of worship have been closed, believers harassed, and priests mistreated. Freedom to practice religion was never extended to the foreign missionaries, who dominated the Christian Church in China. Like other foreigners, most were expelled from China. A few were convicted of espionage and subversion, and were jailed.

The Communists' main effort, however, has been to change old practices gradually through education and by providing beneficial alternatives to old religious practices. For example, better medical facilities and care have greatly reduced reliance on witch doctors; the removal of ancestral remains from family plots to common graveyards has increased the amount of land available for agriculture; and the encouragement of less expensive funerals has lifted a heavy financial burden once considered necessary to honor dead ancestors properly.

In addition, as many people have pointed out, Maoism itself is like a religion in many respects. It has a concept of future paradise (on earth), a savior (Chairman Mao), a set of sacred books (Mao's works), saints (revolutionary martyrs), hymns, and proselytizing missionaries (Party cadres). And last, but by no means least, it has a distinct set of moral principles.

In this regard, a statement from the Vatican in Rome in April, 1973, is interesting. It asserts that Maoist doctrine contains some directives that "find authentic and complete expression in modern social Christian teaching." The statement goes on to say that "Christian reflections" are present in the thoughts of Mao, and that present-day China, like Christianity, "is devoted to a mystique

71

of disinterested work for others, to inspiration by justice, to exaltation of simple and frugal life, to rehabilitation of the rural masses, and to a mixing of social classes." °

Obviously there are many important differences between Christianity and Maoism, but the Catholic Church finds in Maoist moral principles the basis for reconciliation between the Vatican and the People's Republic.

As a demonstration of the analogy between Maoism and religion, consider the following poem. It was written in 1969 when the cult of Maoism was at its height in China.

In what ways could this poem be considered religious?

Long Life to You, Chairman Mao

Over the surging waters
Of the great Yangtse,
Ten thousand *li*, and more,
Rises a bright red sun,
Riding over the waves,
Shaking the earth!
The bold and stately mountains
Straighten out;
The rippling waters
Sing a joyful song:
Chairman Mao!
Our most respected and beloved leader
Chairman Mao
Enjoys good health;
Enjoys good health!
Chairman Mao
You give us
Faith and strength illimitable;
With your encouragement
Comes the realization of our great ideals;

° Reported in the *New York Times*, April 18, 1973.

Seaborne Cultural Work Team, Kwangchow, from *Chinese Literature*, No. 4 (Peking: Foreign Languages Press, 1969).

We give of our best,
Aim high;
We will follow you forever!
We will advance
Through storm and hurricane!
We bless you, Chairman Mao;
Long, long life to you.

Long Life to You, Chairman Mao

The cult of Mao was particularly a feature of the early years of the Cultural Revolution, 1966-1976, when the aging leader made his most vigorous attempt to transform the habits and traditional thought patterns of the Chinese people. Mao's works became, for a short while, almost the sole reading material available to the Chinese people. No work on any topic was published without obligatory quotations from The Chairman.

Since the death of Mao in 1976, his role in the Chinese revolution has been reassessed. As the following excerpt from a 1980 article in a communist Party journal indicates, the cult of Mao has been repudiated. Is it still possible to consider communism a religion or at least a substitute for religion? ह&

Opposing Personality Cult

Is it possible for the Party Central Committee to make mistakes? Is it possible for responsible comrades of the Central Committee to make mistakes? Yes, it is in both cases.

In the late 50s, due to lack of normal, democratic life inside the Party, and due to lack of properly conducted criticism and self-criticism, the responsible comrade of the Central Committee (Chairman Mao) deviated from his own correct thinking and made mistakes. For many years ... the personality cult prevailed, so that a particular person was deified and it was assumed that whatever he said or did was one hundred per cent correct and there couldn't possibly be any doubt about it

There were many other things that smack of feudalism and ignorance, things like: he understands the situation to the last detail, he sees right through everything, and he is our saviour.

The consequences of this were: firstly, democratic centralism which is a Party tradition disappeared completely; secondly, it was utterly impossible to seek truth from facts; thirdly, it was utterly impossible to emancipate the mind; and fourthly, it inevitably led to feudal autocracy under which one person had all the say and patriarchal practices prevailed and this was exploited by some bad elements, who engaged in fascist practices.

So the personality cult, something which is so completely anti-Marxist, must be repudiated in all seriousness and it must never be revived again in future.

Meng Hsiang-ying Stands Up

With the rise of the peasant movement, the women in many places have now begun to organize rural women's associations; the opportunity has come for them to lift up their heads . . . .

Mao Tse-tung, 1927

≤§ *Editor's Introduction:* We have seen the importance of land reform and thought reform in revolutionary China. We have also seen how the Communists have tried to change the traditional Chinese family, rejecting the old family ethic as the basis of social morality. The Communists insist that the interests of the family should not take precedence over the interests of the society at large.

In addition, they have taken steps to alter relationships and behavior within the family. This is particularly true in regard to the role of women. The changed status of women in China today is one of the most remarkable differences between the new and the old China.

The next selection begins by describing some of the "old rules" that regulated the lives of women and goes on to illustrate how the status of women changed. The story takes place in the 1940's, during the war with Japan. The heroine, Meng Hsiang-ying, lives in a village in a Communist-controlled area. Other areas were controlled by the Japanese and still others by the Chinese Nationalist government of Chiang K'ai-shek.

"Meng Hsiang-ying Stands Up," by Zhao Shuli, translated by W. J. F. Jenner. From *Modern Chinese Stories,* © Oxford University Press, 1970, pp. 121-38; abridged.

How does Meng Hsiang-ying successfully rebel? What similarities do you notice between the movement for land reform, as described in "Stone Wall Village Turns Over" and "The Paupers' Co-op," and the movement for women's liberation?&

THIS IS WILD hill-country: As they used to say in the old days, "the mountains are high and the emperor is far away," which could be brought up to date as "The mountains are high and the government is far away"—it is some fifteen miles to the district government office. For this reason the customs here have not changed much since the last years of the Ch'ing dynasty [19th century]. For women the old rule still holds good that as a daughter-in-law you have to put up with beating and abuse, but that once you become a mother-in-law yourself you can beat and curse your daughter-in-law. If you don't, you're failing to put up a good show of being a mother-in-law. The old rule for men in handling their wives is, "A wife you've married is like a horse you've bought—you can ride them or flog them as you like." Any man who does not beat his wife is only proving that he is afraid of her. . . .

One day Meng asked her mother-in-law for some cloth with which to patch her husband's clothes, and the mother-in-law told her to ask the father-in-law for it. According to the old rules she should not have had to ask him for patching cloth, and when Meng argued the point with her mother-in-law, leaving her without a leg to stand on, the mother-in-law started abusing her again. The mother-in-law, realizing that she could not possibly win against Meng, who was in the right and prepared to argue, hurried to the fields to call her son.

"Mei-ni" (this was Meng's husband's name), "come back at once. I can't do anything with that young madam of yours. She wants to eat me alive."

As she could not control the young madam, Mei-ni had to come back and flaunt his authority as young master. The moment he arrived he grabbed a stick and went for Meng—according to the old rules there was no need for him to bother to ask why. But Mei-ni did not have much authority himself, being a lad of only sixteen and a year younger than his wife, and Meng snatched the stick back from him.

This caused real trouble. By the old rules, when a man beat his wife she was expected to take a few blows and then run away, after which somebody else would take the stick from him and that would be the end of the matter. But Meng had not simply refused to be beaten and to run away, she had actually disarmed him, making him feel thoroughly humiliated. In his rage he picked up a sickle and hacked a bloody wound on Meng's forehead, from which the blood kept gushing out even after they had been pulled apart.

The people who broke up the fight seemed to think that Mei-ni had done wrong. Nearly everyone said that if he had to hit her, he should have done so anywhere but on the head. They were only saying that he had hit her in the wrong place. Nobody asked why he had hit her. By the old rules there was no need to ask why a man had hit his wife.

After the fight everyone dispersed as though it were no business of theirs. The only person not to take so casual an attitude was Meng herself. If her head had been cut open when she was completely in the right, and nobody was going to say a fair word for her, then it seemed that there was nothing to stop her husband from hitting her whenever he wanted to. Was this to go on forever? The more she thought about it the more hopeless it seemed. Finally she decided on suicide and swallowed some opium.

As she did not swallow enough she did not die but started retching violently. When her relations discovered this they poured some dirty water, in which combs had been cleaned, down her throat, which made her bring it all up.

"If you like swallowing opium that's fine," her mother-in-law said. "I've got a whole jar of it. I hope you can swallow the lot." Meng would have been glad to, but her mother-in-law did not produce it. . . .

In 1942 a [Communist Party] worker came [to the village]. When he asked them to choose a leader for the Women's

National Salvation Association the villagers suggested Meng. "She can talk," they said, "and that means she can keep a firm grip on what is right." But nobody had the courage to discuss the proposal with her mother-in-law. "I'll go myself," said the worker, but he met with some opposition. "She won't do," said Meng's mother-in-law. "She's a failed suicide, she couldn't cope. . . ."

The worker, a young man, lost his patience when all his arguments were met with "she couldn't cope" by Meng's mother-in-law. "If she can't," he shouted, "then you'll have to." To his surprise this did the trick. Meng's mother-in-law had always thought that being a village cadre was dangerous, because sooner or later you were bound to get shot by [Chiang K'ai-shek's] 40th Army. The reason why she did not want Meng to be one was not so much out of love for her as that she was afraid of being in trouble herself as a cadre's relation. This was why, after all her refusals, the worker's suggestion that she should do it herself threw her into a panic. She would get into less trouble by having her daughter-in-law as a cadre than by being one herself. So she became much more amenable: "It's none of my business, none at all. If she can cope, let her."

The worker had won. From then on Meng headed the Women's Association.

As a village cadre she had to go to meetings. Meng would say to her mother-in-law, "Mother, I'm going to a meeting," and off she would go. Mother-in-law was astonished at the idea of a young woman going to a meeting, but she could not stop Meng for fear that the worker would make her take the job on herself. . . .

Meng's mother-in-law had mixed feelings about women taking part in meetings. She would have liked to go along and have a look but decided she had better not; if she did, [Chiang K'ai-shek's] 40th Army would say when they came that she had gone to meetings organized by the "[Communist] 8th Route faction." The next day her curiosity made her go along to find out what a lot of young women together talked about at a meeting. Her investigations shocked her. The women wanted emancipation; they were against being beaten and sworn at by their mothers-in-law and husbands; they were for ending foot-binding; they wanted to gather firewood, fetch water, and till the fields; they wanted to do the same work and eat the same food as the men; they wanted to go to winter school.

In her view, this was rebellion. If mothers-in-law and husbands could not beat young wives, who would? Surely someone had to beat them. Meng had feet that she would not allow her mother-in-law to bind small enough, no matter how she was beaten and cursed; surely she did not have the nerve to demand that they be allowed to grow bigger still. Would women who gathered firewood and fetched water still be women? Meng was uncontrollable enough while illiterate, but if she learned to read and write she'd be even more high and mighty. What was the world coming to?

Meng was not particularly bothered by her mother-in-law's worries. With the worker's help her job ran smoothly. She went to a lot of meetings and frequently attended winter school. When a young wife was beaten by her mother-in-law or bullied by her husband, she told Meng, who told the [Communist Party] worker. Then there would be meetings, criticism, and struggle. . . .

No matter what everyone else thought, Meng's mother-in-law was developing a stronger and stronger dislike for her. . . . In her view, a daughter-in-law should be like this: her hair should be combed as straight as a broom handle and her feet should be as small as lotus-leaf cakes; she should make tea, cook, husk millet, mill flour, offer soup and hot water, sweep the floor, and wipe the table clean. From the moment when she started the day by emptying the chamberpots till she set the bedding out at night, she should be at her mother-in-law's beck and call, without wandering off for a single moment. She should hide whenever she saw a stranger, so that outsiders would never know you had a daughter-in-law unless you told them yourself.

This was how she felt daughters-in-law should be, even

though she had not always lived up to it in her own youth. She felt that Meng was getting further and further from being a model daughter-in-law. . . . Instead of discussing things with her mother-in-law and keeping some of them from the [Communist] worker, she told him everything. As the mother-in-law made this summary, she thought gloomily, "What am I to do? I can't beat her, I can't swear at her, I can't control her, and I can't sell her. She won't regard herself as a member of the family much longer. Anyone would think the worker her own father." After many sleepless nights she finally thought of a solution: to divide the household.

She asked Niu to be the witness to the division. It was a fair one—if it had not been, Meng would probably not have agreed to it. Meng and her husband took two-thirds of an acre of level land and the same amount of sloping land, but they did not get any grain. "It's all been eaten," her mother-in-law said, "because we harvested so little." After the division the

(From *Jen-min hua-pao*, 1971, Nos. 7–8.)

husband went back to his mother's house to eat and sleep, which left Meng free to go her own way by herself.

After the division, in which all the food she got was less than three pounds of turnips, Meng had nothing to eat but the wild plants. As she had no grain at the New Year, she borrowed nearly three pounds of millet, seven of wheat, and one of salt.

As the district government office is some fifteen miles away, they could not oversee work there, and besides, local cadres were very hard to find. The district Women's Association found it most unreasonable that someone as good as Meng was, both at working herself and at organizing others to beat famine, should be driven from home and left to go hungry. Besides, it hindered work throughout the district. They asked higher authority for permission to issue her with some grain to help her out, and kept her there to organize some of the Women's Association work at the district level.

Meng has been a most successful district cadre this year. . . . In the spring she organized the women to hoe ninety-three acres of wheat and dig two acres of level land as well as seven and a half of hillside. In the struggle against locusts that summer, they cut over ten tons of grass for burning to smoke them out. There is no need for me to go into her other achievements —harvesting wheat, loosening the soil, raking with branches, stripping the twigs of the paper-mulberry tree, and gathering wild plants to eat—because it has all been reported in the press.

Lessons for Women

Editor's Introduction: The story of Meng Hsiang-ying frequently refers to the "old rules." Let us go to an early source of those rules, the famous "Lessons for Women," by Pan Chao, who is sometimes called the most famous woman scholar in China. She wrote the "Lessons" for her daughters in the first century A.D. They were based on customs and values handed down through the centuries, and for nearly two thousand years they continued to be the standard of proper conduct for every young lady. As you read them, try to imagine what a similar essay called "Rules for Men" might prescribe.

HUMILITY

ON THE THIRD day after the birth of a girl, the ancients observed three customs: (1) to place the baby below the bed; (2) to give her a potsherd with which to play; and (3) to announce her birth to her ancestors by an offering. Now, to lay the baby below the bed plainly indicated that she is lowly and weak and should regard it as her primary duty to humble herself before others. To give her potsherds with which to play signified that she should practice labor and consider it her primary duty to be industrious. To announce her birth before her ancestors

Pan Chao, "Lessons for Women," in Nancy Lee Swann, *Pan Chao, Foremost Woman Scholar of China* (New York: Russell and Russell, 1968), pp. 82–90; abridged. Copyright © 1932 by Princeton University Library. Reprinted by permission.

Chinese women, photographed in the nineteenth century.
(From G. W. Browne and N. H. Dole, *The New
American and the Far East,* Boston, 1907.)

clearly meant that she ought to esteem as her primary duty the
continuation of the observance of worship in the home.

These three ancient customs epitomize a woman's ordinary
way of life and the teachings of the traditional ceremonial rites
and regulations. Let a woman modestly yield to others; let her
respect others; let her put others first, herself last. Should she
do something good, let her not mention it; should she do
something bad, let her not deny it. Let her bear disgrace; let
her even endure when others speak or do evil to her. Always
let her seem to tremble and to fear. Then she may be said to
humble herself before others.

Let a woman retire late to bed, but rise early to duties; let
her not dread tasks by day or by night. Let her not refuse to
perform domestic duties whether easy or difficult. That which
must be done, let her finish completely, tidily, and systemati-
cally. Then she may be said to be industrious.

Let a woman be correct in manner and upright in character in order to serve her husband. Let her live in purity and quietness [of spirit] and attend to her own affairs. Let her love not gossip and silly laughter. Let her cleanse and purify and arrange in order the wine and the food for the offerings to the ancestors. Then she may be said to continue ancestral worship.

No woman who observes these three [fundamentals of life] has ever had a bad reputation or has fallen into disgrace. If a woman fail to observe them, how can her name be honored; how can she but bring disgrace upon herself?

HUSBAND AND WIFE

If a husband does not control his wife, then the rules of conduct manifesting his authority are abandoned and broken. If a wife does not serve her husband, then the proper relationship [between men and women] and the natural order of things are neglected and destroyed.

RESPECT AND CAUTION

If husband and wife have the habit of staying together, never leaving one another, and following each other around within the limited space of their own rooms, then they will lust after and take liberties with one another. From such action improper language will arise between the two. This kind of discussion may lead to licentiousness. Out of licentiousness will be born a heart of disrespect to the husband. Such a result comes from not knowing that one should stay in one's proper place. . . .

WOMANLY QUALIFICATIONS

A woman [ought to] have four qualifications: (1) womanly virtue; (2) womanly words; (3) womanly bearing; and (4) womanly work. . . .

To guard carefully her chastity; to control her behavior; in every motion to exhibit modesty; and to model each act on the best usage—this is womanly virtue.

To choose her words with care; to avoid vulgar language; to speak at appropriate times; and not to weary others [with much conversation] may be called the characteristics of womanly words.

To wash and scrub filth away; to keep clothes and ornaments fresh and clean; to wash the head and bathe the body regularly, and to keep the person free from disgraceful filth may be called the characteristics of womanly bearing.

With wholehearted devotion to sew and to weave; to love not gossip and silly laughter; in cleanliness and order [to prepare] the wine and food for serving guests may be called the characteristics of womanly work.

These four qualifications characterize the greatest virtue of a woman. No woman can afford to be without them. In fact they are very easy to possess if a woman only treasure them in her heart. The ancients had a saying: "Is love far off? If I desire love, then love is at hand!" So can it be said of these qualifications.

Wholehearted Devotion

Now in the "Rites" is written the principle that a husband may marry again, but there is no Canon that authorizes a woman to be married the second time. Therefore it is said of husbands as of Heaven, that as certainly as people cannot run away from Heaven, so surely a wife cannot leave [a husband's home]. . . .

The ancient book "A Pattern for Women" says: "To obtain the love of one man is the crown of a woman's life; to lose the love of one man is to miss the aim in woman's life."

Implicit Obedience

Whenever the mother-in-law says, "Do not do that," and if what she says is right, unquestionably the daughter-in-law obeys. Whenever the mother-in-law says, "Do that," even if what she says is wrong, still the daughter-in-law submits unfailingly to the command.

Let a woman not act contrary to the wishes and the opinions of parents-in-law about right and wrong; let her not dispute with them what is straight and what is crooked. ., . .

The Status of Women
Old Customs, New Laws

Editor's Introduction: The "Lessons for Women" clearly indicate the inferior status of women in traditional China, but they do not tell the whole story. The following selection describes some of the other disadvantages of being born female. It also indicates some of the steps that have been taken to bring about change, and why the Communists have had great support from women in promoting revolution.

THE CLEAREST INDICATION of female subservience in traditional China was the bizarre custom of footbinding. It began in about the tenth century A.D. and continued for a thousand years, until the middle of the present century. There are many theories about the original reasons for footbinding, but no one seems to know how it began. Whatever the origin, small feet became an obsession with Chinese men.

Well-bound feet were about three inches long. They made women walk with an unusual swaying motion that Chinese men found very attractive. The stigma attached to large feet was such that every woman, no matter what her social level (except in a very few areas of China), had her feet bound. Grandmother Ning, a working woman who had been a beggar

By Peter J. Seybolt.

for part of her life, described the binding of her feet in an interview:

> They did not begin to bind my feet until I was seven because I loved so much to run and play. Then I became very ill and they had to take the bindings off my feet again. . . .
>
> When I was nine they started to bind my feet again and they had to draw the bindings tighter than usual. My feet hurt so much that for two years I had to crawl on my hands and knees. Sometimes at night they hurt so much I could not sleep. I stuck my feet under my mother and she lay on them so they hurt less and I could sleep. But by the time I was eleven my feet did not hurt and by the time I was thirteen they were finished. The toes were turned under so that I could see them on the inner and under side of the foot. They had come up around. Two fingers could be inserted in the cleft between the front of the foot and the heel. My feet were very small indeed.
>
> A girl's beauty and desirability were counted more by the size of her feet than by the beauty of her face. Matchmakers were not asked "Is she beautiful?" but "How small are her feet?" A plain face is given by heaven but poorly bound feet are a sign of laziness.
>
> My feet were very small indeed. Not like they are now. When I worked so hard and was on my feet all day I slept with the bandages off because my feet ached, and so they spread.*

Bones that resisted the pressure of the bandages were broken by a blow from a wooden mallet. It is not surprising that the feet of many girls and women became diseased, and death was not an uncommon result.

Footbinding had been on the decline for a number of years before the Communists came to power. Westerners had been very critical of the practice since the 1800's, and this seems to have influenced the Chinese. Chiang K'ai-shek's government outlawed footbinding but had been unwilling or

---

* A Daughter of Han, the Autobiography of a Chinese Working Woman, as told to Ida Pruitt by Ning Lao T'ai-t'ai (Stanford: Stanford University Press, 1967), p. 22. Originally published by Yale University Press and used by permission.

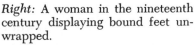

Right: A woman in the nineteenth century displaying bound feet unwrapped.

Above: A comparison of a bound foot and a normal foot.

unable to stop it completely. It ended very quickly after 1949.

The Communists also forbade and put an end to female infanticide—the practice of exposing newborn baby girls to the elements and letting them die, resorted to by impoverished families, usually during a famine, when they could not feed all of the family members. Boys were almost never killed, because only males could perform the all-important rites of ancestor worship and because they, in their privileged status, could better provide security for their parents in old age.

Female slavery was another institution maintained for centuries before the Communists came to power. Poor families often sold their daughters to the rich. The family that owned a slave was obligated to contract a marriage for her when she came of age and to free her at that time. Not infrequently, slave girls became concubines (second, third, or fourth wives) to wealthy men. The children they bore always belonged legally to the first wife and the father.

Some of the slave girls were sold into prostitution. In traditional China, every town of any size had its licensed "tea house" prostitutes. Shanghai, a city built by Westerners seeking fortune and adventure in China, had many thousands of prostitutes. The Communists closed down the "fiery pits" that exploited these girls and established rehabilitation centers, where they were taught a trade and cured of venereal disease, which was rampant among them.

The former prostitutes were treated as unfortunate victims of the old society and foreign imperialism, not as sinful degenerates or enemies of society. According to the Chinese press and reports of foreign travelers, there are no prostitutes in China today. It is probably the only country in the world where that is true.

Although female infanticide, slavery, and prostitution were very common in traditional China, most girls and women escaped those circumstances. But all were subject to the tyranny of the mother-in-law and the legal domination of the husband. Because the Communists promised women freedom and complete equality, it is not surprising that women played a very important role in the revolution.

When the Communists came to power in 1949, one of the first laws the new government passed was the "Marriage Law," which made women legally the equals of men. The provisions of this law leave no room for doubt that past customs and attitudes are no longer acceptable.

The Marriage Law

[Promulgated by the Central People's Government on May 1, 1950.]

CHAPTER I. GENERAL PRINCIPLES

Article 1. The arbitrary and compulsory feudal marriage system, which is based on the superiority of man over woman and which ignores the children's interests, shall be abolished.

The new democratic marriage system, which is based

on free choice of partners, on monogamy, on equal rights for both sexes, and on protection of the lawful interests of women and children, shall be put into effect.

Article 2. Bigamy, concubinage, child betrothal, interference with the remarriage of widows, and the exaction of money or gifts in connection with marriage shall be prohibited. . . .

CHAPTER III. RIGHTS AND DUTIES OF HUSBAND AND WIFE

Article 7. Husband and wife are companions living together and shall enjoy equal status in the home.

Article 8. Husband and wife are in duty bound to love, respect, assist, and look after each other, to live in harmony, to engage in production, to care for the children, and to strive jointly for the welfare of the family and for the building up of a new society.

Article 9. Both husband and wife shall have the right to free choice of occupation and free participation in work or in social activities.

Article 10. Both husband and wife shall have equal right in the possession and management of family property.

Article 11. Both husband and wife shall have the right to use his or her own family name.

Article 12. Both husband and wife shall have the right to inherit each other's property.

Women in China today are equal to men according to the law, but true equality has not yet been realized. Women are supposed to receive equal pay for equal work, but often they do not. More boys than girls attend school at the higher levels, and many more men than women occupy positions of responsibility in government, in production, in schools, and so on.

But no women in the world have come so far in so short a time as have the women of China. And in no other country is women's liberation promoted so vigorously today.

The Home Life of a Saleswoman

≈§Editor's Introduction: The next selection appeared in the Chinese journal *China Reconstructs*. It gives a picture of what life is like for at least one woman in China today. As you read it, pay attention to what the writer thinks is important. Note particularly her relationship with her husband and the values she reveals when discussing the upbringing of her children. How does her life compare with that of salespeople you know? How does her family life compare to family life in the United States?§≈

BOTH MY HUSBAND and I work in the Peking Department Store, the city's largest. My husband, Wang Chun-chuan, is on the management staff. I work behind the counter. We have three daughters. The older two, aged ten and eight, are in primary school. The youngest, 4, goes to the nursery run by the store. Although both of us work and we have children, we have all along been able to work with our minds free from domestic worries and have never needed to let housework and having children affect our progress.

FINDING A JOB

Since liberation, not only do the women of new China enjoy political equality, but an increasing number of them have left the confines of the home to take on jobs in all fields. One day in 1956, when I was sixteen, I came into town from the out-

Tsui Hsiu-mei, "A Saleswoman's Home Life," *China Reconstructs*, January, 1973, pp. 32–34.

skirts and heard that the department stores were advertising for shop assistants. I plucked up courage and applied, not really expecting to be taken on, but I was accepted. When I went home and told the family, my father was much moved. "You're living in good times, daughter," he said. "In my day, even men had a hard time getting a job of any kind, to say nothing of girls like you."

When I reported for work I was put on the "trainee shift." It was explained to me that this was for rather young beginners like myself. We were to work seven hours instead of the regular [eight-hour] shift while still getting the full pay. That would enable us to get more rest and to study more.

MARRIAGE

I found my work very interesting and put all my energy into becoming a good saleswoman. I moved into the living quarters for single women staff-members and after work would get together with my girl friends to chat, sing or read.

I love basketball and spent a lot of time on the court in the yard. I took part in almost every match, either against another department in the store or as a member of our store's team in city tournaments. That was how I met Wang Chunchuan, also a basketball fan. We found we had a lot in common besides basketball. We often did our political reading together, and we found we were very close together in our thinking. Temperamentally we suited each other too. An affection grew up between us, and in 1962 we were married.

Several months after our marriage I became pregnant. As a worker in a state enterprise I am covered by National Labor Insurance. Once a month, later once every two weeks, I could take time out from work for a checkup. From my seventh month of pregnancy, I worked seven instead of eight hours, with no cut in pay. My baby was born in the hospital with which our company has a contract, with all expenses for delivery and hospitalization, except for meals, paid by the Labor Insurance Fund. I had fifty-six days of maternity leave with pay.

MOTHERHOOD

Life became more complicated after I became a mother, but the main problem of child care was solved by the crèche of the nursery run by our store, which is not very far from where we live. There are four classes in the nursery: At fifty-six days, infants can enter the nursing class. When a child is one and a half years old, he goes on to the lower class; at three, he goes on to the middle class; and at five, he goes on to the higher class. When the child is seven years old, he leaves to go on to primary school.

Either Chun-chuan or I took the baby to the nursery on our way to the store and picked her up after work every day. According to the regulations, I was permitted to take half an hour off twice a day, in the morning and afternoon, to run over to the crèche to nurse the baby. This went on until she was weaned. When our daughter was one and a half years old, we put her in the full-time nursery—that is, she lived there all week and came home to us for Saturday night and Sunday. We could go and visit her any time we wanted. In this way I needed to worry even less about the child.

Chun-chuan earns sixty-eight *yuan* [1 *yuan* equals about $.50 U.S. today] a month and I get fifty-five. When our daughter was in the day crèche, was paid six *yuan* a month for her care and an additional sum for food, which included milk and fruit. When she started going full time, we paid fifteen *yuan* a month, which covered everything, including food. The rather low fee is possible because the company subsidizes the nursery out of its workers' welfare fund.

When my first child entered the nursery, I worried about this and that. But after I learned all about the nursery, I felt that my worries were unnecessary. The nurses are patient and affectionate. The children get regular health checkups and all the necessary preventive inoculations. Clothes and bedding are washed and changed regularly. During the hot summer days, the children are given baths every day. Particularly after the age of three, attention is paid to various aspects of character education, such as honesty, love of labor, and an attitude of caring for public property.

All three of my daughters grew up in the nursery. Beginning collective life at a very early stage, they have developed good habits and are all in good health. While they were in the nursery, I did not have to be bothered when they had light

Tsui Hsui-mei and her family. (From *China Reconstructs*, January, 1973, p. 33.)

illnesses, as these were attended to by the nursery health-worker. When the trouble was more serious, they called me at the store and I would be given time off to take the child to the clinic. Sometimes if we happened to be very busy, the nursery staff would do this for me. Last autumn I was sent to the far outskirts of the city to interview job applicants. A few days after I left, my youngest daughter suddenly ran a high fever. A member of the nursery staff immediately took her to the clinic and called my husband to say that she had done so.

HOUSEHOLD TASKS ARE SHARED

Since Chun-chuan and I both work, we don't want to spend much time cooking. Usually we have breakfast and supper at home and eat our lunch in the staff dining room. Quite often we buy cooked rice or steamed bread at the dining room and come home and cook one or two vegetable or meat dishes that we like. This saves much time and enables us to eat in a home atmosphere more often. When we are busy, we sometimes eat all three meals in the dining room, and our two older daughters come to join us.

On Sunday, when the whole family gets together, we usually have some special dishes. Chun-chuan and the children go to the market and select some fish, a family favorite, or we all pitch in and make *jiaozi* (filled dumplings), a treat for the children. Since Chun-chuan is a good cook he frequently prepares the food while I do the laundry or mending. After lunch, the children usually clamor to go to the park or to see a film. We generally follow their wishes and take them out.

Chun-chuan and I share the daily housework. The two older girls are beginning to take quite a bit of it off our hands. They have one characteristic in common: they are diligent and love labor. They fight to go on little errands, such as running to the store for things like soy sauce or vinegar. There were quite a few funny incidents while the older child was learning to cook rice. Once she put the rice on the stove and then went out to play. . . . By the time she thought of the rice, the whole potful was scorched. When I saw it I didn't know whether to laugh or cry.

"Who's going to eat this rice?" I said weakly.

"Well, Mama, you're always telling us not to waste grain . . ."

In the end we all ate it.

We make it a point not to spoil the children and do our best to cooperate with the school in character education and cultivating in them a thirst for knowledge. The girls all try to do as Chairman Mao teaches, "Study well and make progress every day."

On National Day last year, my cousin took my second daughter to the park. The girl saw a fountain pen lying on the grass. She picked it up and called out, "Whose fountain pen is this?" When no one answered, she dragged my cousin out of the park with her, found a policeman and handed the pen to him to be placed at the lost-and-found center.

The oldest girl is very capable at housework. She does her own laundry and sometimes that of her sisters. She helps them wash their hair. On Saturday afternoon, she often goes and fetches her youngest sister from the nursery, so that my husband or I do not have to do it.

Of an evening we like to look through the day's *People's Daily* to keep up with important international and domestic affairs. Sometimes we turn on the radio and listen to music or operas. I spend some of the time studying Marxist-Leninist classics and Chairman Mao's writings. All my colleagues are making a serious study of these and I have to work extra hard to keep up, because I did not have as many years of schooling as most of them. Chun-chuan helps me a good deal. When we were studying the *Communist Manifesto*, he found some background material for me to read and discussed the more difficult points with me. He often recommended newspaper articles in which people who had studied the *Manifesto* told what they had got out of it.

Our household arrangements enable us to give our full attention to our work. If someone at the store happens to be out sick and there is no substitute available, I can easily put in extra hours, and it always gives me a good feeling to be able to contribute a little more to the building of socialism, however small my part.

Romance in the New China

≈§Editor's Introduction: It's not all work for young people in the countryside or elsewhere in China, though one might get that impression from reading Chinese publications. Youth in China are just as romantic and just as attracted to members of the opposite sex as are young people all over the world. But they don't talk about it as much as we do. Nor are they bombarded by advertising that plays on sexual interest to sell products.

The Peking saleswoman we read about, Tsui Hsiu-mei, says she met her husband at a basketball game. They did political reading together (studying the works of Chairman Mao) and were very close in their thinking. Such is the standard testimony of young couples in China when asked about their marriages.

Foreigners traveling in China who inquire about courtship customs and relations between the sexes are often met with a shy, embarrassed response. A Japanese journalist in Shanghai asked a twenty-five-year-old woman about her concept of an ideal husband. He reports that she blushed violently and answered in a trembling voice, "A man who devotes his heart and soul to the task of serving the people of the whole world as is described in Chairman Mao's *In Memory of Norman Bethune*." That reply might have been contrived for a nosy foreigner. The girl might have given a very different response to a close friend. On the other hand, she might have been perfectly sincere. Her answer would sound ridiculous elsewhere in the world, but in China, no one would find it odd.

The Chinese have one of the lowest divorce rates in the world.

Wang Wen-shih, "Summer Nights," *Women of China*, Nos. 4–5, 1960, pp. 45–48; abridged.

Why? Is it because common attitudes toward politics and work bind husbands and wives together? Perhaps. At any rate, politics seems to be a prominent feature of family life in China.

One looks almost in vain for love poetry or stories about romance in Chinese publications. When they appear, sexual attraction is only implicit or suggested. The explicit or obvious theme is a lesson in politics or the proper attitude toward labor. The story you are about to read, which appeared in 1960 in the journal *Women of China*, illustrates this point. How does it differ from other romantic literature you have read?

EVERY DAY AT dusk, as the village bell rang for the last time and stars began to appear in the summer sky, a young man would silently emerge through the twilight. Slung over his shoulder was a purple haversack.

He had an air of serious preoccupation not usually found in one so young. Each time he arrived, he would greet the two girl tractor-drivers with his confident attractive smile and put down his haversack. Then he would walk up to the tractor and examine its mechanism from every angle with his flashlight, asking no end of questions, like a master technician. Even when the tractor was in operation he would walk along with it, watching every movement of the driver. He would give the driver a helping hand whenever she needed one, carrying an oil can or getting boiled water. . . . Sometimes he would make some entries in his notebook, after which he would lie down for a rest not far from where the girls had erected their tent. When the village bell sounded at dawn, he would rise, take up his haversack, and smile farewell at the girls. But the same day at dusk, he would punctually appear again. . . .

Ma Yun-yun, a sweet and saucy-faced lass, born and raised on a farm, had learned to drive a tractor after only three days' instruction and had become an advanced driver. Her manner was definitely cool to the comings and goings of this young man. In the past few days, she had complained several times to her team-mate, Hsu Yu-chin, who was also her teacher and chief of their tractor team.

"I really don't understand. Why are you so friendly to him? Who is he, anyway?"

"I don't know," Yu-chin replied apologetically. She was a sweet-faced girl with fair skin and a full figure. "Anyway, he is a young man of our commune."

"Fine! You don't even know him. A girl who's going to be married any day—why don't you send him away?"

The two girls, . . . having finished their breakfast, went to the river. Their precious tractor stood on the flats below. Suddenly, they were startled to hear the roar of the tractor engine. With Yun-yun in the lead, the girls raced down the path. On the dyke beside the lotus pond, Yun-yun abruptly halted.

"Look, Yu-chin! There he is again! It's all because you were too easy on him!". . .

Yun-yun charged to the northern end of the field directly in the path of the approaching tractor. The machine halted. Yun-yun saw for the first time in daylight the face of the "criminal" in the driver's seat. She was very surprised. The glowing sunrise clouds lit up a handsome, sunburned visage. A pair of honest, determined black eyes glanced back at the turned soil, then gazed at Yun-yun, as if expecting her approbation.

"Come down!" the girl commanded. But her tone wasn't as brusque as she had intended it to be.

With an apologetic smile, the young fellow leaped down from the seat.

"It isn't enough that you hang around all night. You have to come in the daytime too!"

"This is my day off."

"If it is, why don't you go someplace and rest? Why come here?"

The young man's face fell.

"What you've been doing is illegal, don't you know?" She spoke with a serious air, conscious of the fact that she was from the first batch of tractor-drivers, but still a naughty girl for all that.

With startled eyes, the young fellow looked at Yun-yun, then at the tractor, then at the approaching Yu-chin.

"I don't think I've hurt it," he mumbled.

The sight of this large, brawny youth, so utterly cowed by a mere slip of a girl a head shorter than he, struck Yu-chin as very funny. She had been intending to criticize him severely, but now she only said in a firm but pleasant voice: "You must never do anything like this again. If we're going to bring mechanization to the countryside, we have to observe some rules and discipline."

After silently considering this for a moment, the young fellow smiled and said frankly: "I was wrong. Check over your machine, then tell me what I should do."

"Of course I'll check it!" she said to him sternly. She made a thorough examination of the tractor, finally climbing into the driver's seat, starting up the engine. Only then did she solemnly wave her hand to Yu-chin to indicate that nothing was wrong with the machine.

Concealing her amusement at Yun-yun's antics, the older girl said to the young man: "Let's have no more of this monkey business. If you want to learn, come around to our station after the summer planting is over."

The young man thanked her, then looked at Yun-yun with a provocative smile that seemed to say: So you thought you could scare me! We'll see about that!

Yun-yun raised her chin. "I'll let you go this time."

With a farewell glance at the tractor, the young fellow picked up his haversack and strode toward the river flats, a smile still lurking at the corners of his mouth. . . .

The broad fields of the bottom of the land rolled away to the east like waves, and the tractor sailed over them. Yun-yun, who had just completed the afternoon shift, decided not to return to Aunt Wang's [where she was staying while she worked in that area.* She decided instead] to sleep in a lean-to set up against the wall of a small temple. The day was over and the sun was setting over the Wei River. One section had been newly ploughed. She appraised it with an expert eye.

---

* "Aunt" is a term of respect and affection applied to an older woman; Yun-yun and Aunt Wang are not related.

"Terrific!" she muttered admiringly. "Yu-chin's done over ten acres in one shift!" This girl who so loved work and new accomplishments, couldn't restrain her enthusiasm. The blood in her veins sang, her spirits soared.

"Hey! Hey! Hey!" She cried through the night to Yu-chin on the tractor.

"Hey! Hey! Hey!" The echo rang back across the river flats, much to Yun-yun's delight. She heard her youthful voice from the echo.

She shouted again, wildly, and again came an echoing call. Only in addition to the sound of her own voice, there was another—ardent, vibrant, strong. Startled, she peered through the mist.

"Oh, my! Who in the world have I woken up by shouting."

Someone was coming toward her across the field, closer and clearer. Halting at the lean-to, he addressed Yun-yun cheerfully, like an old friend.

"Is it our fine land that makes you so happy?"

That bulging purple haversack again, that gay confident manner!

"What are you doing here?" Yun-yun asked in surprise. "Coming to practice on our tractor again?"

"You needn't worry, comrade. I've just come back. I hear there's a party here tonight and I want to see if it's ready yet or not."

"A party? Last time when you messed around with our tractor, you were having a day off. Tonight, you've come to a party. You must think we're running some kind of a club!"

The young man grinned. "You often don't believe my words. Well, wait and see."

He shouldered his haversack and walked away to the west.

Not long after, Aunt Wang came, bringing food for the girls. Yu-chin drove up with the tractor and said to Yun-yun: "The Youth League is giving a party tonight. We're both invited."

(From *China Reconstructs*, September, 1973.)

"There really is a party?" said Yun-yun, remembering the young man's words. "Why didn't you tell me before?"

A bright pressure lamp was hanging high on the pole of the lean-to, brilliantly illuminating a section of the dark fields.

The young men of the village, the girls, the young wives, arrived chatting and laughing. They greeted the girl tractor-drivers and peered with great interest at the machine.

At that moment, a man came forward through the crowd. Catching sight of him, Aunt Wang cried happily: "So you're back, Shu-hung!"

Yu-chin looked up in surprise when she heard him addressed as Shu-hung: . . . the young man who had stealthily driven their tractor was Aunt Wang's son, a childhood friend whom Yun-yun had not seen for years. . . .

The party went on happily beneath the starry summer-night sky. There was lively music, voices of songs, happy laughter. As if inspired by this youthful merriment, the waters of the ancient Wei murmured a rhythmic accompaniment. . . .

Shu-hung and Yun-yun, shoulder to shoulder, strolled through the fields, recalling the hardships of their childhood, talking of their interests and their plans.

Yun-yun couldn't understand why she felt so close to this young man. She kept asking herself—when she had scolded him so severely and practically chased him away, had she liked him? . . . He was so determined, so persistent, yet so unselfish, so politically aware, so confident! . . .

Many thoughts ran through her mind as she listened to him. Before they knew it, they had reached the white poplar grove. The poplar leaves rustled and danced in the gusty night breeze.

"What's this about you becoming a team-leader?" Yun-yun asked Shu-hung affectionately.

"That's right. It was decided officially only yesterday. Our brigade is going to have its own tractor team. The commune Party committee wants me to take charge. Mother tells me you like our compound," said Shu-hung. . . .

Yun-yun raised her head and met his gaze. How many

questions and answers were exchanged in that brief meeting of eyes as the moonlight filtered through the trees! The usually wild Yun-yun was suddenly mature. The change was so marked that even she was aware of it. Hastily, she turned her eyes away.

In a light, strange voice that was filled with happiness, she said, "The moon has risen. I've got to start my night shift."

They returned through the grove. The moon seemed abruptly to rise higher: the bottom land seemed suddenly to light up and grow broader. Not far beyond the side of the grove, the celebration was going strong. Merrymakers were singing the vigorous chorus of the song about the drivers of tractors. . . .

The Confucian Heritage

꩜ *Editor's Introduction:* If romance in China is affected by politics, so then is everything else, and for 30 years after 1948 the thinking of Mao pervaded Chinese politics and therefore society. But prior to Mao—for a period of 2,000 years—the teaching of Confucius prevailed in China. Indeed, if we could use only one word to describe traditional China, that word would be "Confucian."

Confucianism was a way of life, a philosophy of government, a system of ordering society. Like communism, it pervaded all aspects of human activity. It was not a religion as we usually think of religion. Confucius believed in gods, but he was mainly interested in perfecting life on earth.

What is Confucianism? To answer that question adequately would take years of study. But some understanding of Confucian values can be gained by reading a few fragments of the conversations between Confucius and his disciples, recorded more than 2,500 years ago and compiled in a book called the *Analects*. What values did Confucius emphasize? What similarities and differences do you see between Confucian and Maoist values? ꩜

Regard for the past:

Confucius said: "I am a transmitter and not a creator. I believe in and have a passion for the ancients."

Education:

Confucius said: "By nature men are pretty much alike; it is learning and practice that set them apart."

"Selections from *The Analects*," in W. T. de Bary *et al.* (eds.), *Sources of Chinese Tradition*, Vol. I (New York: Columbia University Press, 1960), pp. 23-33; abridged.

A Confucian official.

Confucius said: "Those who are born wise are the highest type of people; those who become wise through learning come next; those who learn by overcoming dullness come after that. Those who are dull but still won't learn are the lowest type of people."

Humanity:

Confucius said: "Behave when away from home as though you were in the presence of an important guest. Deal with the common people as though you were officiating at an important sacrifice. Do not do to others what you would not want others to do to you. Then there will be no dissatisfaction either in the state or at home."

Confucius said: "To be able to practice five virtues everywhere in the world constitutes humanity. [The five are] courtesy, generosity, good faith, diligence, and kindness. He who is courteous is not humiliated; he who is generous wins the multitude; he who is of good faith is trusted by the people; he who is diligent attains his objective; and he who is kind can get service from the people."

Filial piety [respect for parents]:

Confucius said: "Nowadays a filial son is just a man who keeps his parents in food. But even dogs or horses are given food. If there is no feeling of reverence, wherein lies the difference?"

Religion:

. . . about the worship of ghosts and spirits Confucius said: "We don't know yet how to serve men, how can we know about serving the spirits?" "What about death?" was the next question. Confucius said: "We don't know yet about life, how can we know about death?"

. . . about wisdom Confucius said: "Devote yourself to the proper demands of the people, respect the ghosts and spirits but keep them at a distance—this may be called wisdom."

The gentleman:

Confucius said: "The gentleman is always calm and at ease; the inferior man is always worried and full of distress."

Confucius said: "The gentleman understands what is right; the inferior man understands what is profitable."

Confucius said: "The gentleman makes demands on himself; the inferior man makes demands on others."

Government by personal virtue:

Confucius said: "Lead the people by laws and regulate them by penalties, and the people will try to keep out of jail, but will have no sense of shame. Lead the people by virtue and restrain them by the rules of decorum, and the people will have a sense of shame, and moreover will become good."

Confucius said: "The essentials are sufficient food, sufficient troops, and the confidence of the people." Tzu Kung [a disciple] said: "Suppose you were forced to give up one of these three, which would you let go first?" Confucius said: "The troops." Tzu Kung asked again: "If you were forced to give up one of the two remaining, which would you let go?" Confucius said: "Food. For from of old, death has been the lot of all men, but a people without faith cannot survive."

The Scholar Who Passed
the Examination

Editor's Introduction: The Confucian emphasis on humanity and self-perfection no doubt had an influence on China's rulers and helped to perpetuate the Confucian ethos for so many centuries. Those entrusted with government were supposed to be humane and unselfish, to devote themselves to a lifelong study of moral principles, and to set an example by their own conduct. Their main function as government officials was to maintain the peace and well-being of society.

There were no castes in traditional China. The ruling class was not born to a position of authority like the European or Japanese aristocracy. The highest positions in government were open to any man (women were excluded). Any male with the leisure and the money to pay a tutor could study the Confucian books and could take a series of civil service examinations that would qualify him for government service and high honors. Education, then, was the key to success in Confucian China, and, in theory, everyone had an equal chance.

In fact, however, there was little equality of opportunity. Few people of humble background could afford the many years of study required to learn the very difficult Chinese classical written language (it has been greatly simplified today) and virtually memorize the dozen or so basic Confucian books.

Wu Ching-tzu, *The Scholars* (Peking: Foreign Languages Press, 1964), pp. 67–77; abridged.

Furthermore, once a person had passed the exams and was awarded a degree he was elevated to a position infinitely higher than that of the common people. He was guaranteed wealth, power, and status. Confucian society erected a rigid barrier between "gentlemen" and "small men." The gentlemen were "mental workers" who governed the small men and were supported by them. They disdained any sort of physical labor. The long gowns they wore and their long fingernails, which sometimes reached six inches, were symbols of their nonlaboring status. It is in an effort to destroy this tradition and the attitudes of superiority and disdain for working people it produces that Mao Tse-tung has insisted that all students, intellectuals, and government officials engage in physical labor together with working people.

In Confucian China, it was not just custom but also law that kept class distinctions clear. One's social rank determined the kind of clothes he could wear, the size of his house, and the kind of food he could eat. Criminal laws were not applied equally to the great and the small. In a law suit between people of the two classes, it was assumed that the gentleman, with his extensive moral training, was the innocent party. If he was found guilty, his sentence for most crimes would be lighter than that for a man of lower status found guilty of the same crimes. In short, Confucianism did everything possible to maintain class distinctions, to keep everyone in his place. Only in this way, Confucius taught, could peace and harmony be maintained.

The story that follows, written in the eighteenth century, pokes fun at aspects of the Confucian system by exaggerating them. Like all good satire, it is based on reality. As the story opens, a number of students are going into an examination hall. From there they will go into small individual rooms, or cells, to write.

What, specifically, is the story criticizing? What does it tell you about the Confucian system?⁊❧

THE THIRD EXAMINATION was for candidates from Nan-hai and Pan-yu Counties. Commissioner Chou sat in the hall and watched the candidates crowding in. There were young and old, handsome and homely, smart and shabby men among them. The last candidate to enter was thin and sallow, had a grizzled beard and was wearing an old felt hat. Kwangtung has a warm climate; still, this was the twelfth month, and yet this candidate had on a linen gown only, so he was shivering with cold as he took his paper and went to his cell. Chou Chin made a mental note of this before sealing up their doors. During the first interval, from his seat at the head of the hall, he watched this candidate in the linen gown come up to hand in his paper. The man's clothes were so threadbare that a few more holes had appeared since he went into the cell. Commissioner Chou looked at his own garments—his magnificent crimson robe and gilt belt—then he referred to the register of names, and asked, "You are Fan Chin, aren't you?"

Kneeling, Fan Chin answered, "Yes, Your Excellency."

"How old are you this year?"

"I gave my age as thirty. Actually, I am fifty-four."

"How many times have you taken the examination?"

"I first went in for it when I was twenty, and I have taken it over twenty times since then."

"How is it you have never passed?"

"My essays are too poor," replied Fan Chin, "so none of the honorable examiners will pass me."

"That may not be the only reason," said Commissioner Chou. "Leave your paper here, and I will read it through carefully."

Fan Chin kowtowed and left.

It was still early, and no other candidates were coming to hand in their papers, so Commissioner Chou picked up Fan Chin's essay and read it through. But he was disappointed. "Whatever is the fellow driving at in this essay?" he wondered. "I see now why he never passed." He put it aside. However, when no other candidates appeared, he thought, "I might as well have another look at Fan Chin's paper. If he shows the least talent, I'll pass him to reward his perseverance." He read it through again, and this time felt there was something in it. . . .

Then he read Fan Chin's paper again. This time he gave a gasp of amazement. "Even I failed to understand this paper the first two times I read it!" he exclaimed. "But, after reading it for the third time, I realize it is the most wonderful essay in the world—every word a pearl. This shows how often bad examiners must have suppressed real genius." Hastily taking up his brush, he carefully drew three circles on Fan Chin's paper, marking it as first. . . .

Fan Chin's mother and wife were delighted by his success. They were preparing a meal when his father-in-law arrived, bringing pork sausages and a bottle of wine. Fan Chin greeted him, and they sat down together.

"Since I had the bad luck to marry my daughter to a scarecrow like you," said Butcher Hu, "Heaven knows how much you have cost me. Now I must have done some good deed to make you pass the examination. I've brought this wine to celebrate."

Fan Chin assented meekly, and called his wife to cook the sausages and warm the wine. He and his father-in-law sat in the thatched shed, while his mother and wife prepared food in the kitchen.

"Now that you have become a gentleman," went on Butcher Hu, "you must do things in proper style. Of course, men in my profession are decent, high-class people; and I am your elder too—you mustn't put on any airs before me. But these peasants round here, dung-carriers and the like, are low people. If you greet them and treat them as equals, that will be a breach of etiquette and will make me lose face too. You're such an easy-going, good-for-nothing fellow, I'm telling you this for your own good, so that you won't make a laughing-stock of yourself.". . .

Since it was the year for the provincial examination . . . Fan Chin's fellow-candidates asked him to go with them to the provincial capital for the examination, but he had no money for the journey. He went to ask his father-in-law to help.

Butcher Hu spat in his face, and poured out a torrent of abuse. "Don't be a fool!" he roared. "Just passing one examination has turned your head completely—you're like a toad trying to swallow a swan! And I hear that you scraped through not because of your essay, but because the examiner pitied you for being so old. Now, like a fool, you want to pass the higher examination and become an official. But do you know who those officials are? They are all stars in heaven! Look at the Chang family in the city. All those officials have pots of money, dignified faces, and big ears. But your mouth sticks out and you've a chin like an ape's. You should piss on the ground and look at your face in the puddle! You look like a monkey, yet you want to become an official. Come off it! Next year I shall find a teaching job for you with one of my friends so that you can make a few taels [ounces] of silver to support that old never-dying mother of yours and your wife—and it's high time you did! Yet you ask me for traveling expenses! . . .

When [Fan Chin] got home again, he thought to himself, "Commissioner Chou said that I showed maturity. And, from ancient times till now, who ever passed the first examination without going in for the second? I shan't rest easy till I've taken it." So he asked his fellow candidates to help him and went to the city (without telling his father-in-law) to take the examination. When the examination was over he returned home only to find that his family had had no food for two days. And Butcher Hu cursed him again.

The day the results came out there was nothing to eat in the house, and Fan Chin's mother told him, "Take that hen of mine to the market and sell it; then buy a few measures of rice to make gruel. I'm faint with hunger."

Fan Chin tucked the hen under his arm and hurried out.

He had only been gone an hour or so when gongs sounded and three horsemen galloped up. They alighted, tethered their horses to the shed, and called out: "Where is the honorable Mr. Fan? We have come to congratulate him on passing the provincial examination."

Not knowing what had happened, Fan Chin's mother had hidden herself in the house for fear. But when she heard that he had passed, she plucked up courage to poke her head out and say, "Please come in and sit down. My son has gone out."

"So this is the old lady," said the heralds. And they pressed forward to demand a tip.

In the midst of this excitement, two more batches of horsemen arrived. Some squeezed inside, while the others packed themselves into the shed, where they had to sit on the ground. Neighbors gathered round, too, to watch; and the flustered old lady asked one of them to go to look for her son. The neighbor ran to the marketplace, but Fan Chin was nowhere to be seen. Only when he reached the east end of the market did he discover the scholar, clutching the hen tightly against his chest and holding a sales sign in one hand. Fan Chin was pacing slowly along, looking right and left for a customer.

"Go home quickly, Mr. Fan!" cried the neighbor. "Congratulations! You have passed the provincial examination. Your house is full of heralds."

Thinking this fellow was making fun of him, Fan Chin pretended not to hear and walked forward with lowered head. Seeing that he paid no attention, the neighbor went up to him and tried to grab the hen.

"Why are you taking my hen?" protested Fan Chin. "You don't want to buy it."

"You have passed," insisted the neighbor. "They want you to go home to send off the heralds.'

"Good neighbor," said Fan Chin, "we have no rice left at home, so I have to sell this hen. It's a matter of life and death. This is no time for jokes! Do go away, so as not to spoil my chance of a sale."

When the neighbor saw that Fan Chin did not believe him, he seized the hen, threw it to the ground, and dragged the scholar back by main force to his home.

The heralds cried, "Good! The newly honored one is back." They pressed forward to congratulate him. But Fan Chin brushed past them into the house to look at the official announcement, already hung up, which read: "This is to announce that the master of your honorable mansion, Fan Chin, has passed the provincial examination in Kwangtung, coming seventh in the list. May better news follow in rapid succession!"

Fan Chin feasted his eyes on this announcement and, after reading it through once to himself, read it once more aloud. Clapping his hands, he laughed and exclaimed, "Ha! Good! I have passed." Then, stepping back, he fell down in a dead faint. His mother hastily poured some boiled water between his lips, whereupon he recovered consciousness and struggled to his feet. Clapping his hands again, he let out a peal of laughter and shouted, "Aha! I've passed! I've passed!" Laughing wildly, he ran outside, giving the heralds and the neighbors the fright of their lives. Not far from the front door, he slipped and fell into a pond. When he clambered out, his hair was disheveled, his hands muddied, and his whole body dripping with slime. But nobody could stop him. Still clapping his hands and laughing, he headed for the market.

They all looked at each other in consternation, and said, "The new honor has sent him off his head!"

His mother wailed, "Aren't we out of luck! Why should passing an examination do this to him? Now he's mad, goodness knows when he'll get better."

"He was all right this morning when he went out," said his wife. "What could have brought on this attack? What *shall* we do?"

The neighbors consoled them. "Don't be upset," they said. "We will send a couple of men to keep an eye on Mr. Fan. And we'll all bring wine and eggs and rice for these heralds. Then we can discuss what's to be done. . . ."

The Scholar Who Passed
the Examination

⊷§Editor's Introduction: The first part of "The Scholar Who Passed the Examination" is a Chinese version of the Horatio Alger story, so familiar to Americans—the poor boy who becomes a success through his own ingenuity and effort. But as the story continues, the plot loses its resemblance to the Horatio Alger theme and becomes more typically Chinese.

What are the differences between the traditional Chinese and American ways of rewarding success?§⊷

"I HAVE AN IDEA," said one of the heralds, "but I don't know whether it will work or not."

"What idea?" they asked.

"There must be someone the honorable Mr. Fan usually stands in awe of," said the herald. "He's only been thrown off his balance because sudden joy made him choke on his phlegm. If you can get someone he's afraid of to slap him in the face and say, 'It's all a joke. You haven't passed any examination!' —then the fright will make him cough up his phlegm, and he'll come to his senses again."

They all clapped their hands and said, "That's a fine idea.

117

Mr. Fan is more afraid of Butcher Hu than of anyone else. Let's hurry up and fetch him. . . ."

One of the neighbors hurried off in search of the butcher and presently met him on the road, followed by an assistant who was carrying seven or eight catties of meat and four or five strings of cash. Butcher Hu was coming to offer his congratulations. Fan Chin's mother, crying bitterly, told him what had happened.

"How could he be so unlucky!" exclaimed the butcher. They were calling for him outside, so he gave the meat and the money to his daughter and went out. The heralds put their plan before him, but Butcher Hu demurred.

"He may be my son-in-law," he said, "but he's an official now—one of the stars in heaven. How can you hit one of the stars in heaven? I've heard that whoever hits the stars in heaven will be carried away by the King of Hell, given a hundred strokes with an iron rod, and shut up in the eighteenth hell, never to become a human being again. I daren't do a thing like that.". . .

[Eventually], Butcher Hu had to give in. Two bowls of

*Butcher Hu about to restore
Fan Chin to his senses.*

wine bolstered up his courage, making him lose his scruples and start his usual rampaging. Rolling up his greasy sleeves, he strode off toward the market, followed by small groups of neighbors.

Fan Chin's mother ran out and called after him, "Just frighten him a little! Mind you don't hurt him!"

"Of course," the neighbors reassured her. "That goes without saying."

When they reached the market, they found Fan Chin standing in the doorway of a temple. His hair was tousled, his face streaked with mud, and one of his shoes had come off. But he was still clapping his hands and crowing, "Aha! I've passed! I've passed!"

Butcher Hu bore down on him like an avenging fury, roaring, "You blasted idiot! What have you passed?" and fetched him a blow. The bystanders and neighbors could hardly suppress their laughter. But although Butcher Hu had screwed up his courage to strike once, he was still afraid at heart, and his hand was trembling too much to strike a second time. The one blow, however, had been enough to knock Fan Chin out.

The neighbors pressed round to rub Fan Chin's chest and massage his back, until presently he gave a sigh and came to. His eyes were clear and his madness had passed! They helped him up and borrowed a bench from Apothecary Chen, a hunchback who lived hard by the temple, so that Fan Chin might sit down.

Butcher Hu, who was standing a little way off, felt his hand begin to ache; when he raised his palm, he found to his dismay that he could not bend it. "It's true, then, that you mustn't strike the stars in heaven," he thought. "Now Buddha is punishing me!" The more he thought about it, the worse his hand hurt, and he asked the apothecary to give him some ointment for it.

Meanwhile, Fan Chin was looking round and asking, "How do I come to be sitting here? My mind has been in a whirl, as if in a dream."

The neighbors said, "Congratulations, sir, on having passed the examination! A short time ago, in your happiness, you brought up some phlegm; but just now you spat out several mouthfuls and recovered. Please go home quickly to send away the heralds."

"That's right," said Fan Chin. "And I seem to remember coming seventh in the list." As he was speaking, he fastened up his hair and asked the apothecary for a basin of water to wash his face, while one of the neighbors found his shoe and helped him put it on.

The sight of his father-in-law made Fan Chin afraid that he was in for another cursing. But Butcher Hu stepped forward and said, "Worthy son-in-law, I would never have presumed to slap you just now if not for your mother. She sent me to help you."

"That was what I call a friendly slap," said one of the neighbors. "Wait till Mr. Fan finishes washing his face. I bet he can easily wash off half a basin of lard!"

"Mr. Hu!" said another. "This hand of yours will be too good to kill pigs any more."

"No indeed," replied the butcher. "Why should I go on killing pigs? My worthy son-in-law will be able to support me in style for the rest of my life. . . ."

When they reached Fan Chin's house, Butcher Hu shouted: "The master is back!" The old lady came out to greet them and was overjoyed to find her son no longer mad. The heralds, she told them, had already been sent off with the money that Butcher Hu had brought. Fan Chin bowed to his mother and thanked his father-in-law, making Butcher Hu so embarrassed that he muttered, "That bit of money was nothing."

After thanking the neighbors too, Fan Chin was just going to sit down when a smart-looking retainer hurried in, holding a big red card, and announced, "Mr. Chang has come to pay his respects to the newly successful Mr. Fan."

By this time the sedan-chair was already at the door. Butcher Hu dived into his daughter's room and dared not come out, while the neighbors scattered in all directions. Fan Chin went out to welcome the visitor, who was one of the local gentry, and Mr. Chang alighted from the chair and came in. He was wearing an official's gauze cap, sunflower-colored gown, gilt belt, and black shoes. He was a provincial graduate, and had served as a magistrate in his time. His name was Chang Chin-chai. He and Fan Chin made way for each other ceremoniously, and once inside the house bowed to each other as equals and sat down in the places of guest and host. Mr. Chang began the conversation.

"Sir," he said, "although we live in the same district, I have never been able to call on you."

"I have long respected you," replied Fan Chin, "but have never had the chance to pay you a visit."

"Just now I saw the list of successful candidates. Your patron, Mr. Tang, was a pupil of my grandfather; so I feel very close to you."

"I did not deserve to pass, I am afraid," said Fan Chin. "But I am delighted to be the pupil of one of your family."

After a glance round the room, Mr. Chang remarked, "Sir, you are certainly frugal." He took from his servant a packet of silver, and stated, "I have brought nothing to show my respect except these fifty taels of silver, which I beg you to accept. Your honorable home is not good enough for you, and it will not be very convenient when you have many callers. I have an empty house on the main street by the east gate, which has three courtyards with three rooms in each. Although it is not big, it is quite clean. Allow me to present it to you. When you move there, I can profit by your instruction more easily."

Fan Chin declined many times, but Mr. Chang pressed him. "With all we have in common, we should be like brothers," he said. "But if you refuse, you are treating me like a stranger." Then Fan Chin accepted the silver and expressed his thanks. After some more conversation they bowed and parted. Not until the visitor was in his chair did Butcher Hu dare to emerge.

Fan Chin gave the silver to his wife. When she opened it, and they saw the white ingots with their fine markings, he asked Butcher Hu to come in and gave him two ingots, saying, "Just now I troubled you for five thousand coppers. Please accept these six taels of silver."

Butcher Hu gripped the silver tight, but thrust out his clenched fist, saying, "You keep this. I gave you that money to congratulate you, so how can I take it back?"

"I have some more silver here," said Fan Chin. "When it is spent, I will ask you for more."

Butcher Hu immediately drew back his fist, stuffed the silver into his pocket and said, "All right. Now that you are on good terms with that Mr. Chang, you needn't be afraid of going short. His family has more silver than the emperor, and they are my best customers. Every year, even if they have no particular occasions to celebrate, they still buy four or five thousand catties of meat. Silver is nothing to him."

Then he turned to his daughter and said, "Your rascally brother didn't want me to bring that money this morning. I told him, 'Now my honorable son-in-law is not the man he was. There will be lots of people sending him presents of money. I am only afraid he may refuse my gift.' Wasn't I right? Now I shall take this silver home and curse that dirty scoundrel." After a thousand thanks he made off, his head thrust forward and a broad grin on his face.

True enough, many people came to Fan Chin after that and made him presents of land and shops, while some poor couples came to serve him in return for his protection. In two or three months, he had menservants and maidservants, to say nothing of money and rice. When Mr. Chang came again to urge him, he moved into the new house; and for three days he entertained guests with feasts and operas. On the morning of the fourth day, after Fan Chin's mother had got up and had breakfast, she went to the rooms in the back courtyard. There she found Fan Chin's wife with a silver pin in her hair. Although this was the middle of the tenth month, it was still warm and she was wearing a sky-blue silk tunic and a green silk skirt. She was supervising the maids as they washed bowls, cups, plates, and chopsticks.

"You must be very careful," the old lady warned them. "These things don't belong to us, so don't break them."

"How can you say they don't belong to you, madam?" they asked. "They are all yours."

"No, no, these aren't ours," she protested with a smile.

"Oh yes, they are," the maids cried. "Not only these things, but all of us servants and this house belong to you."

When the old lady heard this, she picked up the fine porcelain and the cups and chopsticks inlaid with silver, and examined them carefully one by one. Then she went into a fit of laughter. "All mine!" she crowed. Screaming with laughter she fell backward, choked, and lost consciousness. . . .

The Leakage System

◄§Editor's Introduction: Confucius said: "The gentleman cherishes virtue; the inferior man cherishes possessions." This was the ideal, and there were gentlemen-officials who sacrificed their own well-being and material comfort for the good of the people. But a far more common situation is revealed by the expression, "Become an official and get rich." The story you have just read indicated that a degree-holder, one of the "stars of heaven," invariably received "gifts" from those who hoped to benefit later from this favor.

In the next selection, Chiang Monlin, former Chancellor of Peking University, writing in 1947, describes how some officials under the traditional system acquired a fortune. What changes had to be made in the traditional Chinese system of government to eliminate this "leakage"?§►

FROM THE GOVERNMENT offices through which public revenues passed, the government required only certain fixed amounts to be forwarded to the national treasury. The officials in charge of the revenues could, by various means and all sorts of excuses and plausible reasons, attach a variety of fees to the regular taxes. In this way, for every *tael* of silver that flowed into the government treasury, at least the same amount or even more would be diverted to "leakage" funds. In the later years of the imperial regime, more wine leaked into private cups than remained in the public barrel. The government, find-

Chiang Monlin, *Tides From the West* (Taipei: China Culture Publishing Foundation, 1957), pp. 160–64; abridged.

ing itself parched as a fish in a dry pond, pressed hard for more money—whence still more "leakage" for public servants and heavier burdens for the people. . . .

But as to the "leakage" system and how it worked. China was then divided into some twenty-two provinces, comprising about two thousand *hsien* [counties]. The chief executive of the *hsien* was the magistrate, who took charge of all financial matters and concurrently filled the role of administrator of justice in his district. His salary—not more than a few *taels* a month—was nominal. All expenses incurred by the holder of the office had to be paid out of "leakage" funds. When higher officials of the imperial government passed through his district, he had to entertain them and secure for them all the "necessities" required for their travel. To the entourage of any higher official he had to offer "presents," usually in the form of money.

On the banks of the Yao-kiang River, just outside the city wall of my native Yu-yao, stood a welcome pavilion at which the magistrate welcomed passing officials of higher rank. One sunny afternoon some forty years ago, I noticed crowds gathering at a distance from the pavilion. I joined them and watched the landing of the Imperial Examiner and his entourage, on their way to Ning-po to hold civil examinations in that prefecture. On the previous day, the magistrate had "caught," or requisitioned, many houseboats from the people, and the one set aside for the Imperial Examiner was loaded with sealed cases, their contents known only to those who had prepared them.

I watched the party change boats. The Imperial Examiner stepped into the most prominent; the sails were set and the little flotilla with the officials and "leakage" gifts on board floated downriver with the ebbing tide to the seaport city of Ning-po. Under that inspiration, I said to myself that from now on I must study hard, so that some day I myself might be an Imperial Examiner blessed with such mysterious gifts as lay hidden in those cases.

Regular "gifts" had to be presented to the secretaries of the civil governor of the province. Failing that, a magistrate could not expect them to speak kind words for him to the governor and would find them faultfinding in his official relations with the governor's office. Added together, the amount required for plain sailing in his career was by no means small. Human nature also made him not unmindful of the necessity to provide for a rainy day. And he had his family and followers to support.

Candidates for magistracy who had pull were covetous of the districts with large revenues. I remember that in the *hsien* in which we lived during my school days, no magistrate had ever held office for more than a year. The regular term of office was three years, in which a magistrate could realize approxi-

An official at home with his family and servants.

mately a hundred thousand dollars. In those times, this sum was considered very great. So the governor appointed acting magistrates, whose term was usually one year. In this way there would be more chances for expectant magistrates to share the profit.

When a magistrate retired from office after the expiration of his term and paid an official call on the governor, he was usually asked by his superior whether his district had been a good one, meaning how much he had got out of the "leakage" funds. His friends and relatives also asked him the same question by way of starting a conversation.

The higher the rank of the official through whose hands the government revenues passed, the more "leakage" flowed into his private coffer. The *taotai* of Shanghai was known to reap a profit of some 100,000 *taels* a year. Governors and vice-roys of rich provinces and the powerful princes and grand ministers in Peking usually enjoyed large yearly incomes. . . .

The poisonous sap penetrated even to the households of the well-to-do. The cook would poke "holes" in his vegetable and meat baskets in order to make them "leak." Servants got something from the purchases they made for the household—especially in Peking the shops always added a certain percentage to the price for the servants who made the purchase. . . .

The practice of "leakage" permeated the entire system of *likin* [a tax on commerce]. And *likin*, like a gigantic octopus with tentacles reaching to every communication line in the country, sucked the blood out of the trade and commerce of the nation.

It worked this way. Anyone who knew how to "squeeze" the people would bid—say two hundred thousand dollars a year—to government agents for the right to run the *likin* at a certain station or a number of stations established at points on the highway where merchandise passed from one city to another. The person who won the bid would become *likin* commissioner at that station or group of stations and had the right to assess duties on the goods passing through. If he could realize a sum of three hundred thousand dollars within the year, he would turn over two hundred thousand to the government and keep the remainder for himself and his partners. So he would make most goods dutiable in order to swell his private fortune.

Once I saw a boat loaded with watermelons passing under the bridge at a station. It was stopped by a long bamboo hook from shore and several inspectors jumped down and began to thrust iron rods into the melons. The owner begged them to desist and promised to pay any amount they demanded. The "duties" were paid; the poor farmer sailed on.

Editor's Postscript: The "leakage" system of acquiring money was normal and legal in China. Indeed, as the article suggests, it was the only way underpaid officials and others providing services could live. But although custom regulated the amount of "leakage" that was acceptable, and the government removed officials who were especially voracious, the whole system was open to abuse by its very nature, and Confucian morality often exerted little restraint on outright greed. This seems to have been particularly true in the late nineteenth century, when Western power forced a breakdown of Confucian institutions. Customary leakage degenerated into widespread corruption, and this continued into the twentieth century, providing fertile soil for the growth of the Communist movement.

The People's Democratic

Dictatorship

≈§Editor's Introduction: The Communists regard the Confucian system as a dictatorship, meaning that the ruling class was using government power primarily in its own interests. By this definition, Chiang K'ai-shek's government was a dictatorship in support of the landlord class and the new bourgeoisie (the middle class of industrialists and businessmen in the cities). Dictatorship can disappear, the Communists reason, only when there are no classes, when everyone is equal and no one exploits anyone else. To bring this situation about, they say, there must be a "people's dictatorship"—that is, the use of government power in support of the workers and peasants, the great majority of the population, against those who have always oppressed them. Mao Tse-tung explains the concept in an essay he wrote in 1957, reprinted here. What do the terms "democratic centralism," "democratic dictatorship," "freedom," and "discipline" mean as Mao uses them? How would you define such terms as democracy and freedom?§≈

OURS IS A people's democratic dictatorship, led by the working class and based on the worker-peasant alliance. What is this dictatorship for? Its first function is to suppress . . . those exploiters in the country who range themselves against the socialist revolution, to suppress all those who try to wreck our

Mao Tse-tung, *On the Correct Handling of Contradictions Among the People* (Peking: Foreign Languages Press, 1958); abridged.

129

socialist construction; that is to say, to solve the contradictions between ourselves and the enemy within the country.

For instance, to arrest, try, and sentence certain counter-revolutionaries, and for a specified period of time to deprive landlords and bureaucrat-capitalists of their right to vote and freedom of speech—all this comes within the scope of our dictatorship. To maintain law and order and safeguard the interests of the people, it is likewise necessary to exercise dictatorship over robbers, swindlers, murderers, arsonists, hooligans, and other scoundrels who seriously disrupt social order.

The second function of this dictatorship is to protect our country from subversive activities and possible aggression by the external enemy. . . . Should that happen, it is the task of this dictatorship to solve the external contradiction between ourselves and the enemy. The aim of this dictatorship is to protect all our people so that they can work in peace and build China into a socialist country with a modern industry, agriculture, science, and culture.

Who is to exercise this dictatorship? Naturally it must be the working class and the entire people led by it. Dictatorship does not apply in the ranks of the people. The people cannot possibly exercise dictatorship over themselves; nor should one section of them oppress another section. Lawbreaking elements among the people will be dealt with according to law, but this is different in principle from using the dictatorship to suppress enemies of the people. What applies among the people is democratic centralism.

Our Constitution lays it down that citizens of the People's Republic of China enjoy freedom of speech, of the press, of assembly, of association, of procession, of demonstration, of religious belief and so on. Our Constitution also provides that organs of state must practice democratic centralism and must rely on the masses; that the personnel of organs of state must serve the people. Our socialist democracy is democracy in the widest sense, such as is not to be found in any capitalist country. Our dictatorship is known as the people's democratic dictatorship. . . .

[Some people feel that there is] too little freedom under our people's democracy and that there was more freedom under Western parliamentary democracy. They ask for the adoption of the two-party system of the West, where one party is in office and the other out of office. But this so-called two-party system is nothing but a means of maintaining the dictatorship of the bourgeoisie; under no circumstances can it safeguard the freedom of the working people.

As a matter of fact, freedom and democracy cannot exist in the abstract; they only exist in the concrete. In a society where there is class struggle, when the exploiting classes are free to exploit the working people, the working people will have no freedom from being exploited; when there is democracy for the bourgeoisie there can be no democracy for the proletariat and other working people. In some capitalist countries the Communist parties are allowed to exist legally but only to the extent that they do not endanger the fundamental interests of the bourgeoisie; beyond that they are not permitted legal existence. Those who demand freedom and democracy in the abstract regard democracy as an end and not a means. . . .

While we stand for freedom with leadership and democracy under centralized guidance, in no sense do we mean that coercive measures should be taken to settle ideological matters and questions involving the distinction between right and wrong among the people. Any attempt to deal with ideological matters or questions involving right and wrong by administrative orders or coercive measures will not only be ineffective but harmful. We cannot abolish religion by administrative orders; nor can we force people not to believe in it. We cannot compel people to give up idealism any more than we can force them to believe in Marxism. In settling matters of an ideological nature or controversial issues among the people, we can only use democratic methods, methods of discussion, of criticism, of persuasion and education, not coercive, high-handed methods. In order to carry on their production and studies effectively and to order their lives properly, the people want their government, the leaders of productive work and of educational and cultural bodies, to issue suitable orders of an obligatory nature. It is common sense that the maintenance of

Mao Tse-tung and Chou En-lai shortly after the establishment of the new Chinese government. (From Jen-min hua-pao, *1971, No. 10, p. 30.)*

law and order would be impossible without administrative orders. Administrative orders and the method of persuasion and education complement each other in solving contradictions among the people. Administrative orders issued for the maintenance of social order must be accompanied by persuasion and education, for in many cases administrative orders alone will not work. . . .

Leadership and Democracy

The Model Official

✑§*Editor's Introduction:* Under the "people's democratic dictatorship," Chinese workers and peasants participate more in government and in many respects have more voice in determining the course of their lives than ever before. They are encouraged to criticize their government and its officials, especially if the latter are corrupt, inept, or authoritarian. Many cadres have been removed on the basis of mass criticism.

But there are limits to criticism and free speech. The government and the Communist Party do not permit criticism of socialism as a system. And while one can criticize the operation of the Party, no one can question the Party's right to lead. Furthermore, the press and radio are closely controlled by the Party and are vehicles solely for expressing its point of view.

As Mao stated, the Communists believe that restraints on liberty are necessary if Chinese society is really to change. They remind us that the Confucians were even more restrictive of liberty and democracy, for under them the common people had no voice; the overwhelming majority could not even read, much less express themselves freely in print; and the law forbade anyone but officials even to discuss politics.

The following story, which appeared in the journal *Chinese Literature*, published in Peking in 1973, illustrates the balance between leadership and mass criticism that the Communists seek

Yao Keh-ming, "When the Party Secretary Showed Up," *Chinese Literature*, No. 2 (Peking: Foreign Languages Press, 1973), pp. 36–42.

to attain in their system of "democratic centralism." Do you think they succeed? What ideals of leadership are revealed in this fictional account?❧

IT WAS A typical autumn day of mellow sunshine with cloud flecks drifting across the far distant sky. Leaves rustled in a blustery wind.

Two bicycles were bowling along the highway. One of the riders, as she wiped the sweat from her face with a white towel and glanced at her watch, began to speed up. "Get a spurt on, Young Chang! There's only ten minutes left," she called out to the other rider.

This young woman, Miao Chun-min, was a former textile-worker in her early thirties. She looked brisk, neat, and full of pep as she pedaled along with a knapsack slung over her shoulder.

. . . She had recently been elected to the district Revolutionary Committee as a representative of the masses. Later she became the deputy secretary of the district Party committee. Young Chang, also a former factory worker, was transferred to work in the office of the Party committee during the same period.

The two of them were now heading for Green Pines Gardens to keep an appointment with the people living there.

A few days before, while going over the mail, Young Chang had come across a short message written on a slip of paper. In rather crude characters it read:

> Please tell Comrade Miao Chun-min that Green Pines Gardens will welcome a visit from her if she can spare the time. Why is it that we haven't been able to get in touch with her recently? We have tried several times.

This slip of paper had been forwarded by the neighborhood Party committee with a note saying that it had been handed in during a residents' meeting there.

Casually Young Chang had put it away in the file, deciding that some time later he would mention it to Miao. Actually he did not want to bother the deputy secretary with what he considered to be a trifle. Because of the absence of the Party secretary, Miao had been up to her neck in work recently and often stayed up till the small hours. Chang was concerned about her health and, wanting to do what he could to help her, he settled many routine matters himself. . . .

But in spite of her heavy load of work, Deputy Secretary Miao took particular interest in the mail—which was mostly letters from people in the district.

One morning, when looking through a file of letters, she noticed that little slip of paper. Seeing that she paused thoughtfully over it, Young Chang went over to her desk to explain:

"It's just one of those chits people keep handing in. . . ."

"No. It's more than that! It should be taken as a sharp criticism of our work," rejoined Miao. "We so often miss criticism of this sort. We seldom hear it at formal meetings or come across it in reports."

"If everybody in the district wants to talk to the Party secretary, how many more secretaries should we need?" argued Chang.

"It's a good thing if the people want to see us."

"But you're so busy . . . and this is only routine. . . ."

"The busier we are the closer we should keep to the people. . . . Since the people want to see us, we ought to visit them and pay careful attention to what they say," Miao told Chang. "Besides, this visit will help us sum up our experience of local work.". . .

[A meeting is then arranged at Green Pines Gardens, which Miao and Young Chang attend.]

The meeting went on for about two hours in a warm, friendly atmosphere.

After taking a sip of tea, Miao Chun-min looked around and said in a ringing voice, "For the last two hours you've said a great deal in praise of our work. That's an encouragement to us to do better in future." She paused to look around again and then went on with a smile. "But Chairman Mao teaches us that all things have two sides. This applies to our work. To be strict with a person is for his own good. You should make strict de-

mands on the district Party committee, the district Revolutionary Committee, and above all on me as deputy Party secretary. I'm hoping to hear from you where I'm wrong and how I
can correct my mistakes. A person needs to wash his face every
day. . . ."

The people listening nodded and smiled in agreement,
liking her attitude. Then suddenly someone spoke up from a
far corner of the room, "Well, then, let me fire the first shot. If
I'm wide off the mark, you mustn't take offense."

It was Grandma Tung, a retired worker, who spoke. She
had been one of the mainstays of the propaganda team Miao
worked with. Although over sixty and already gray-haired, she
was the picture of health.

"During the past few days I've several times tried to
reach you but failed. I was told either that you had 'some important business' on hand or that you were too busy to 'receive
ordinary calls.' I wonder whether since you've become a leading comrade you've put on bureaucratic airs and forgotten all
about us."

Miao was surprised because nobody had mentioned
Grandma Tung's recent calls and she herself had never said
anything about "important business."

The entire room was silent but everyone was looking at
Secretary Miao. The atmosphere had become a little tense.
. . . [Miao thought to herself]: "The fact that people criticize
me openly and to my face shows that they have my interest at
heart and want to help me. Since I've come here to listen to
what they have to say, I must heartily welcome their criticism
and then try to discover the reason for it." So she jotted down
what Grandma Tung had said, and looking at her modestly
and sincerely said: "Please go on."

Her attitude encouraged Grandma Tung. "I went to your
office on some important business," she continued. "We retired workers have started a group among the residents to
study Marxist ideology and the correct political line. We've
begun by recalling our own bitter experiences in the past and
contrasting them with our good life today. You did say once

A government official (with shovel) heading for work with other peasants. (From China Pictorial, *1970, No. 3, p. 9.)*

that if we started any new activity I should let you know. So I wanted to see you so that you could give us some advice.". . . .

After the old woman had finished, Miao said, "Grandma Tung, I accept your criticism. There's something wrong with my style of work. I have failed to go deep among the people to see what new things are cropping up. Your initiative shows your keen revolutionary spirit. We must learn from you."

These few words like a spring breeze set the entire room astir. People vied with one another for a chance to speak, some giving their opinions and others telling about the new spirit that was emerging among the retired workers and about their political activities. Miao quickly jotted down these vivid accounts, which were full of life. So the gathering turned into a real briefing. Miao was extremely pleased. That "the masses have a potentially inexhaustible enthusiasm for socialism," a truth revealed by our great leader Chairman Mao, was once more being proved true here in Green Pines Gardens.

On the way back after the meeting a question kept revolving in Miao's mind. Why, she wondered, had it become so difficult for an old comrade of hers like Grandma Tung to reach her now? What was the reason?

"Young Chang, what d'you think of the meeting?" Miao asked, turning toward Young Chang, who was cycling beside her.

"It was good, very good, I think. . . ." Young Chang's thoughts were in a turmoil. "It never occurred to me that a short note could involve something so important."

"The note was short but its lesson for us is big." Miao lapsed into deep thought again. After a while she took another look at her comrade and re-opened the conversation in a very frank and sincere way: "This incident has taught me a lot. As one of the leading personnel, any incorrect style of work or political ideology of mine will affect the work and the staff of the whole Party committee."

"No, no, you've nothing to reproach yourself with," protested Young Chang. "I'm the one. . . ." Greatly moved by Miao's attitude, he was at a loss for words.

It was already sunset. Miao glanced back over her shoulder at Green Pines Gardens, now only a green blur against the crimson sky. She said to Young Chang with feeling: "Revolution continually makes higher demands on us. It's true we were both factory workers and can be said to come from the very midst of the people, but we must be careful never to isolate ourselves from them. You know what happens to a pine tree if it is uprooted from the soil."

A Sticky Problem

⁐§ Editor's Introduction: We have seen how the "leakage system" undermined the intentions of Confucianism. The story which follows, "A Sticky Problem," is a witty illustration of how social obligations in China have the same effect on communist ideology.

Like "The Scholar Who Passed the Examination," this story is a satirical treatment of a very real problem in China, namely, the tradition of "taking care" of one's relatives and friends even if it means breaking a few rules here and there. The Communists have spoken out against this practice, but deeply rooted customs are hard to dig out.

The factory director in the story shows extraordinary determination to follow the rules, risking the loss of friends and job. Is he an exception? It would seem that he is.

The author of this story, Wang Meng, is a well-known contemporary Chinese writer. In 1956 he published a short story describing the bureaucratic way of doing things in a district Party committee. The story caused a sensation and a year later Wang Meng was blacklisted and sent "down to the countryside." At that time writers were not free to criticize life in China.

Now that writers enjoy greater freedom in China, Wang Meng has emerged from 20 years of obscurity and is once again expressing his views and enjoying popularity. ₹₩

Excerpted from Wang Meng, "A Spate of Visitors," *Chinese Literature*, Peking, July 1980, pp. 9-21.

Ding Yi Stirs up a Hornet's Nest

At his new post Ding Yi discovered two big problems. Here, the word "discover" is hardly appropriate, because these two problems were as obvious as lice on a bald head. They made him frown and rack his brains every day. First, there was no proper control of the by-product of paste, gluten, which the workers divided among themselves to sell, give to friends or exchange for other goods. This was scandalous. Secondly, the labour discipline was so lax that the foreman sometimes tripped over people sound asleep during their work shifts. So, after consulting everyone concerned, Ding Yi drew up a set of regulations and a system of rewards and penalties. In fact, these were nothing new, just standard practice.

A month went by. In May, Ding Yi decided to make an example of a contract worker named Gong Ding. For one thing, this young man had stayed away from work for four months without asking for leave. For another, he came bold as brass to the factory to demand gluten, and if given none cursed or beat the man in charge. Furthermore, he turned a deaf ear to reprimands. So Ding Yi asked the Party branch committee, Youth League committee, trade union, personnel office and all the other departments to discuss Gong Ding's case. Though he prodded them three times a day, it took them a month and a half to agree to his proposal that this recalcitrant worker should be dismissed. On June 21, an announcement was put up in the factory: In accordance with regulations, Gong Ding's contract is terminated.

Some people knew that Gong Ding was a distant relative of the first county Party secretary Li and felt it was a mistake to fire him, but they did not like to say so. After all, he was only a distant relative. So, the decision was finally reached and announced.

Psychological Warfare Breaks Out

Three hours after the announcement was put up, Ding Yi began to have callers. The first was Old Liu from the county Party committee office. Fifty-seven years old, with an affable expression, he prided himself on his diplomacy and good relations on all sides. Smilingly, he put one hand on Ding Yi's shoulder. "Listen to me, Old Ding," he said. "You've worked hard and run the factory well. But as for Gong Ding's case. . . . " Lowering his voice he explained Gong's relationship to the first county Party secretary. He added, "Of course, this has no bearing on his case. You're right to take disciplinary action. Secretary Li would be grateful to you if he knew. It's you I'm thinking of. You'd better not fire him. He'll still have to stay in China, in our county if he's kicked out. We'll still be responsible for him, and he's bound to ask Secretary Li for help. So, better let him off with a warning." He reasoned so earnestly and patiently that Ding Yi began to waver. Just then, however, Zhou, head of the county industrial bureau, rang up.

"What's come over you?" he bellowed. "Why pick on a relative of the county Party secretary to make an example of? What are people going to think? Hurry up and revoke your decision!"

"No, the decision stands!" replied Ding Yi loudly as he hung up the receiver. His face grim, he turned to Old Liu and said, "Outrageous!"

However, visitors kept coming. At dusk, Old Zhao, chairman of the county revolutionary committee, arrived. Zhao had worked in the county since land reform. He was most influential and strongly entrenched. With a certain reserve he shook hands languidly with Ding Yi, then paced the room while issuing his instructions, not even glancing at Ding.

"We must be prudent, mustn't oversimplify issues. Nowadays people are very sensitive. Gong Ding's dismissal would cause general dismay. In view of this, it's more judicious not to fire him."

He said no more, thinking his directive sufficient. He had paced the room slowly enunciating each word, as if weighing and savouring it. Yes, to him his words were as tasty as spiced beef.

When Ding Yi went home after dark, his wife also poked her nose into his business. Of course, she scolded him out of wifely concern.

"You perishing old fool! Don't you see what you've gone and done? Has messing about with paste all day made you soft-headed? You stick to principles? Why aren't you a member of the politburo? Remember the bashing you got in 1966? Your principles not only got you into trouble but me and the children too."

This outburst stemmed from bitter resentment and love. And the tears she shed were more eloquent than words. Ding Yi sighed, and was just about to reason with her when in came another visitor. It was Young Xiao, who had befriended Ding Yi when he was in disgrace. Young Xiao had studied in the Philosophy Department of Beijing University where he was labelled a Rightist. Later he had managed to get a job in the county's electricity company. Recently, after his name was cleared, he had been promoted to be a buyer. He was short, big-nosed and extremely ugly. But the more pressure put on him, the more cheery, quick-witted and engaging he grew. His motto was: If someone slaps your face, turn the other cheek. He reckoned that this tactic succeeded three times out of four.

Young Xiao's arrival filled the house with laughter. The first thing he did after taking a seat was to finish up the dumplings left by Ding Yi and his wife who had lost their appetite. Then he asked after everyone in the family, saying admiringly, "How lucky you are to have so many relatives." Next he told them that he would soon buy and send over the TV set, a real bargain, they had long wanted. Finally he related various funny stories about their county, China and other countries till the whole family was roaring with laughter . . . .

Young Xiao took advantage of this to launch his offensive. "Why, there's a small matter I nearly forgot," he said. "It's about that young rascal Gong. He's a real shit! I'll dress him down next time I see him. But Old Ding, you mustn't go too far. You and I haven't got much footing here. Nor do we have powerful backing or commodities that other people want. We depend entirely on keeping in with others. Big shots rely on their power, we nobodies on our connections. With power they can get anything they want; by keeping on good terms with others we can make do. So don't be so bull-headed. If you haven't

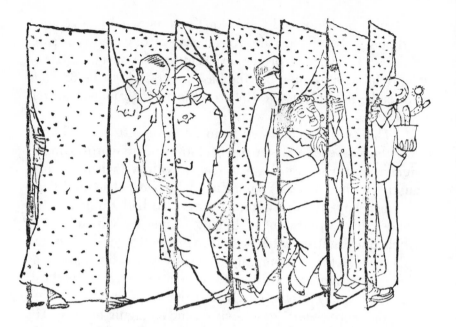

learned anything else all these years, you should have learned
how to veer . . . . I know, you needn't explain it to me. The
decision has been announced; still, it can be changed. Even the
Constitution can be changed, and Chairman Mao made
revisions in his writings. You're only a small factory director.
Think you're more infallible than Chairman Mao and the
Constitution? Go on! Get Gong Ding back. I must make myself
clear. It's not the county secretary who sent me here, I came on
my own initiative, having your interests at heart. Of course,
Gong Ding did ask me to come and I told him, 'Don't you
worry. Old Ding will do me a little favour like this.' "

He certainly had the gift of the gab, able to range from the
sublime to the vulgar, to crack jokes or to scoff.

Originally, Ding Yi had not known that Gong Ding was a
distant relative of the county's first secretary, and he was not
unwilling to reconsider the case. But all these visitors put him
on his guard. If it hadn't been the first secretary's relative,
would so many people have come to urge him to "be prudent",
"not to oversimplify issues" and to "consider the consequences"? This question preoccupied him, to the exclusion of
other considerations.

In his annoyance he sent Young Xiao packing.

Two days passed. June 23, Sunday, was a hot, long mid-summer day. Mosquitoes had kept Ding awake the previous night, and he had no appetite. At half past four that morning, a visitor arrived by bus. He was Ding Yi's brother-in-law. Tall, bespectacled and bald, he had studied in the Marxist-Leninist Institute in the 1950s and was now teaching in the prefectural Party school. He was the best known theorist in the prefecture and enjoyed great prestige. When listening to his lectures, grassroots cadres kept nodding their heads just like chickens pecking millet from the ground. He was the seventeenth visitor in the past two days. As soon as he set foot in the room, he began to talk from a theoretical point of view.

"Socialist society is a transition period in which there exist the scars of capitalism and pre-capitalism. They are inevitable and independent of man's will. This society is superior but not yet mature or perfect. It's only a transition . . . . " After this abstract preamble, he continued:

"So we say, leaders' power, their likes and dislikes, their impressions, are of vital importance. They cannot be overlooked and very often play the decisive role. We are realists, not .

utopian socialists like Owen and Fourier." (Ding Yi thought: Am I a utopian socialist? This label doesn't sound too bad.) "We are not children or pedants. Our socialism is built on the ground under our feet, which, though beautiful, is rather backward and undeveloped." (Ding Yi thought: Have I ever wanted to fly to paradise?) "So when we do any work, we must take all factors into consideration. To use an algebraic formula, there are 'N' factors, not one. The more complicated the world is, the larger the 'N' . . . . So, brother, you were too hasty in handling Gong Ding's case. You didn't use your brain." (Ding Yi thought: A fine brain *you* have, holding forth like this!) "Don't make a gross error, brother, Be statesmanlike. Cancel your decision and invite Gong Ding back."

Ding Yi's wife hastily put in, "That's right, that's right!" A pleased smile appeared on her face. It dawned on Ding Yi that she had asked her theorist brother to talk him round.

While listening, Ding Yi had felt as if his chest was stuffed with hog bristles. His face looked as if he was swallowing a worm. After he had listened attentively for forty minutes, he simply asked, "Did you teach these theories in your Party school?"

Within the twenty-one hours from the arrival of the theorist till 1:45 the next morning, visitors kept coming and going. Some let loose a flood of eloquence, as if they could bring the dying back to life. Some blustered as if they would swallow up the whole world. Some bowed and scraped like swinging willow branches. Some had a well-thought-out plan which they enunciated a word or two at a time, determined not to desist till their goal was reached or, failing that, to hurl Ding Yi over a cliff rather than leave his family in peace. Some brought with them presents ranging from flowers to rancid bean curd. Some promised him a flat with a southern exposure or a brand-new bicycle. Some warned him that he was isolating himself and would come to no good end. Some spoke of the need to protect the Party's prestige—to save the first secretary's face. Some worried about his safety and the fate of his family, some about preserving unity in the country, yet others about human rights, democracy and freedom.

These visitors included Ding Yi's old colleagues, schoolmates, superiors, subordinates, comrades-in-arms, fellow patients in hospital, fellow sufferers, "wine-and-meat" friends and the descendants of his late friends. Some of them were aged people with high prestige, others were promising young ones. Even those who had been in favour of his decision in the factory came over to state that they had changed their minds. Although their motives and manner of speaking differed, they agreed on one point: Gong Ding must not be fired.

Ding Yi had never thought he knew so many people and was known to so many. He could not understand their keen concern for Gong Ding or why his disciplinary action against a contract worker, a hooligan and a distant relative of the county secretary had stirred up such a hornet's nest. He was fast becoming a public enemy! He could neither eat nor rest, nor do any chores. His Sunday was spoilt. He wanted to scream, to smash things, to beat someone up. But instead he gritted his teeth and listened impassively warning himself, "Keep cool and you'll win through!"

Among the visitors was a star whom Ding Yi had admired when young. Forty years ago, she had been the best known actress in the province. And Ding Yi in his teens was infatuated for a spell with this woman thirteen years older than himself, although they did not know each other. He had never told anyone of his romantic dream. It was only in the Cultural Revolution when he was undergoing "labour reform" that he had the luck to meet her, an old lady who had retired and now weighed more than eighty kilograms. Due to his oriental, old-fashioned devotion, Ding Yi had always had a special affection for her. To his surprise this "queen" of earlier times also arrived by a donkey cart that day. Sitting on the bed, she prattled through the gaps in her teeth:

"I should have come to see you earlier, Young Ding. Look at me, aren't I an old witch? I don't know why I've aged so suddenly. Why do so many things come to an end before they've really started? It's like the stage: you're still making up when the music for the final curtain sounds . . . . "

Her lamentation over the transience of life made Ding Yi's eyes moist with tears. Of all his visitors that day she seemed to him the only one who had called on him out of pure friendship. But what she went on to say took him aback:

"I hear you're a real martinet. That's no way to run a factory. It turns people against you, doesn't it? Do unto others as you would be done by. Haven't you learned anything from your own experience? You'd better not be too hard on young people."

Still, Ding Yi was grateful to her, recalling his youthful dreams. Among the visitors that day, she was the only one who made no mention of Rose-fragrance Paste Factory, Gong Ding and the county secretary.

Some Statistics

I hope readers will excuse me if now I depart from the normal narrative style to publish some correct but well-nigh unbelievable statistics.

In the 12 days from June 21 to July 2, the visitors who came to plead for Gong Ding totalled 199.5 (the former actress didn't mention his name but had him in mind, so she is counted in as 0.5). 33 people telephoned. 27 wrote letters. 53 or 27% really showed keen concern for Ding Yi and were afraid he would run into trouble. 20 or 10% were sent by Gong Ding; 1 or 0.5% by Secretary Li. 63 or 32% were sent by people approached directly or indirectly by Secretary Li. 8 or 4% were asked by Ding Yi's wife to talk round her "die-hard" husband. 46 or 23% were not sent by anyone and did not know Ding Yi but came on their own initiative to do Secretary Li a service. The remaining 4% came for no clear reasons.

Ding Yi refused all his visitors' requests. His stubbornness enraged 85% of them, who immediately spread word that he was a fool. Ding Yi's petty appointment had gone to his head, they claimed, making him stubborn and unreasonable, and cutting him off from the masses. They asserted that he was fishing for fame and credit, that he had ulterior motives and was taking this chance to vent his spite because the county Party committee had not promoted him to a higher position.

Some said he was crazy and had always been reactionary, that he should never have been rehabilitated. Assuming that each of them spoke to at least ten people, 1,700 heard talk of this kind. For a while public opinion was strongly against him. It seemed all were out for his blood. His wife fell ill and her life was only saved by emergency measures. Even the nurse in charge of the oxygen cylinder took the chance to ask Ding Yi to change his mind.

Incidents of this kind happen quickly and end quickly too. They are like the breakfast queues in restaurants, which form as soon as fried cakes and porridge are served and disperse immediately after the food is sold out, no matter how angry those balked of fried cakes are. By August there was no further talk of the case, and by September it had escaped people's minds. Meanwhile, the production in the paste factory had gone up each day. By October, great changes had taken place. When talking together, people stuck up their thumbs saying, "Old Ding Yi really knows a thing or two!"

By December, the fame of the paste factory really had the fragrance of roses. It had become a model for all the small enterprises in the province. The Rose-fragrance Paste it produced was consistently of first-rate quality. Ding Yi went to attend a meeting in the provincial capital at which he was asked to report his experience. He went on to the rostrum, his face flushed, and said, "Communists are made of steel, not paste . . . ."

This caused a general sensation.

He added, "If we don't get down to business, our country's done for!"

He broke off there, choking, and tears ran down his cheeks.

There was a solemn silence for a moment in the auditorium.

Then, thunderous applause!

Dissent in the

People's Republic

⇜§*Editor's Introduction:* When they came to power, the Communists exercised their "people's dictatorship" by telling the middle class, particularly the intellectuals (a term the Chinese use to identify those with a high school education or above—probably no more than 5 per cent of the population in 1949), "We welcome your help, we need your talents, if you are willing to help us build socialism. If not, we will deprive you of the right to spread your ideas." The majority of the middle class and the intellectuals went along, some of them, perhaps, with grave reservations or the feeling that there was no alternative. A few who were especially dissatisfied managed to leave China. Such was the case of Robert Loh, a businessman educated in America, who found the new China intolerable and fled to the United States in 1954. His account of his experiences, *Escape from Red China,* was published in the United States in the late 1950's and gained a sympathetic hearing from many Americans. The following selection is an excerpt from that book.

How might Loh's family background have affected his decision to leave China?⇜

WHEN I MADE UP my mind to escape, I knew that I would have an obstacle from within myself. If I were successful, I would

Robert Loh, *Escape from Red China* (New York: Coward-McCann, 1962), pp. 15–36; abridged.

be leaving forever the one place on earth where I belonged. Such a step is painful for anyone, but I think that my background gave me a special attachment to Shanghai.

My parents typified Shanghai's peculiar combination of the ancient and modern. My father, for example, was a deeply religious Buddhist, but he was also fond of American jazz; he once even won a cup in a Charleston contest. Again, although he was a serious classical scholar and had come from a long line of famous scholars, he made his living as an investment broker.

The extreme contrasts of the city were also exemplified in my parents. No two people could have been more unlike. My father's family had had social standing but little money. My mother had been the beautiful spoiled daughter of the *nouveau riche*. My father preferred simplicity, but my mother tended to ostentation. One time, I remember, a friend told her that Madame Chiang K'ai-shek had a pair of hose that cost $18; my mother immediately stated that *she* had a pair costing $24. She wanted the best clothes, the largest mansion, the most lavish parties, and the biggest cars. My father always rode the streetcar to work, he ate only vegetarian food, and his study was starkly furnished.

Like Shanghai itself, however, my parents' differences were harmoniously blended. My father, for instance, indulged my mother in her whims and cooperated fully in the social life she loved. Meanwhile, she saw to it that he had time each day, alone and undisturbed, for study and meditation. Moreover, we spent part of each summer at a Buddhist monastery retreat, and my mother always acted as though she enjoyed it. Despite their differences, they united in lavishing attention and affection on their children.

I was born in November, 1924, the second of three sons. Later we had a baby sister, who was the family favorite. We lived in a Western-style mansion with a huge enclosed garden. We were raised in the Chinese style, however, with a large group of relatives and servants who were like family members, and we had little contact with outsiders.

My first real contact with outsiders came from four White Russian bodyguards hired by my father. The guards were big, simple men who enjoyed our children's games as much as we did. We regarded them affectionately, but in those days White Russians in Shanghai performed the most menial and degrading labor; in Chinese, the word "Russian" came to mean anything that was the shoddiest of its kind. From an early age, I thought that the worst possible fate was to become, like the Shanghai Russians, a despised refugee in a foreign land.

The other Shanghai foreigners were indirectly responsible for our needing the guards. The city was dominated by British and French, but the government was corrupt. Officials often cooperated with gangsters, with whom kidnapping was a common form of extortion. My mother was too lively for the restrictions of being adequately guarded and was kidnapped twice. Fortunately, the gangsters rarely harmed their captives, nor did they demand exorbitant ransom. The payments were made with police connivance. We children suffered terrible shock when our mother was taken. I hated gangsterism and blamed it on the foreigners.

My worst childhood shock, however, came in 1936, when I was almost twelve. Our baby sister died. The effect on my parents was disastrous. In his grief, my father lost interest in his business; he made some wrong investments and lost almost all his money. This additional catastrophe was too much for my mother, and within a few months she also died. Her relatives tended to blame my father—at least, he believed they did, and certainly thereafter they treated him coolly. My father and his sons were drawn closely together. He gave us even more attention and affection. Moreover, although he was only thirty-two, he never remarried. He threw himself into his work. He wanted to obtain for us the material comforts that, I think, he felt he owed to our mother.

The effect of all this was to make me dissatisfied with our class. We had to give up our mansion and all extravagance, but we were not so poor that we endured real hardship. Nevertheless, our relatives humiliated us and our friends abandoned us.

*China in the 1940s—revolution for whom? (Photo by
Silk, from* Life Magazine © *1946 Time, Inc.)*

We felt alone in a hostile world. I came to scorn the values of
the rich. . . . By the time I entered the university, I was in
the group of serious students. Among my classmates, those
with the sophistication to go to nightclubs, drink, and have
affairs with women were admired and envied, but the few of
us who really studied were given genuine respect.

The respect I earned was increased by the fact that the
famous Dr. Stewart Yui, head of the Political Science Depart-

ment, took personal interest in me. He invited me to his house with the advanced students so that I could hear expert discussions on the subject. He made me read political science books not included in the course. Above all, he encouraged me to formulate and express my own ideas. I came to admire him as much as I did my father; more important, through his help I experienced an awakening of self-confidence.

My self-confidence was boosted further by the fact that my father's fortunes were slowly improving. His success, oddly enough, came largely from the confused conditions. By now World War II had started. After Pearl Harbor, all Westerners were interned, and Western business interests were taken over by the Japanese. Business conditions were chaotic. Inflation was uncontrollable, and black-marketing was everywhere. The vaguest rumor caused the stock market to fluctuate wildly. Most businessmen speculated to keep ahead of inflation, and investment brokers therefore were busy. My father refused to handle the more dubious speculative deals. Thus his profits were low but his business was more stable. As his reputation for honesty grew, the number of his clients increased, and finally he commanded a good share of the investment trade.

My father himself continued to live, as always, with spartan frugality, but he shared his new prosperity lavishly with his employees and his sons. My allowance grew until I found that I was receiving as much money as the sons of the richest industrialists. I began entertaining my few friends in the best restaurants, and soon I attracted the attention of the playboy set. . . .

Dissent in the

People's Republic

PART II

⊸§*Editor's Introduction:* Robert Loh became a Shanghai playboy during the war with Japan, when Shanghai was occupied by the Japanese and thousands of residents of the city were dying of malnutrition and disease. After the war, in 1947, he came to the United States and enrolled as a graduate student at the University of Wisconsin. But he seems not to have studied much, for he bought himself "a large Buick Roadmaster with innumerable gadgets" and continued his life as a playboy. His frequent companion was a Chinese named Charlie Chan, the son of "a man of formidable wealth whose textile and flour mills were spread all over China."

Loh describes life with Charlie in the United States as a continual binge.

> Charlie drove me to Chicago in his magnificent Lincoln. At the hotel, everyone seemed delighted at Charlie's arrival; he strode through the place passing out large tips, and we were whisked up to a luxurious suite. After changing, we set off on a tour of the night clubs. . . . He would rent the most impressive limousine available and give the chauffeur a large tip. Thereupon, the chauffeur's duty was to see that we were provided with the best that the city offered in the way of entertainment. By the middle of 1948, I had what was, in effect, a road map to loose living in America.

Robert Loh, *Escape from Red China* (New York: Coward-McCann, 1962), pp. 166–74; abridged.

Soon after the Communists came to power, Robert Loh and Charlie Chan returned to China and entered business. Then their troubles began, as the following selection indicates. The Communists conducted a number of "Thought Reform" campaigns to change the ideas of businessmen and intellectuals in an effort to get them to cooperate actively in building socialism.

In the following selection, Robert Loh describes his experience with Thought Reform. What methods did the Communists use to deal with opposition and gain cooperation? What other methods might they have used?&

Everyone classed as an intellectual prepared an autobiography that began at the age of eight and concentrated on the ideas he had had during his lifetime. Each paper, then, was studied by the other members of the author's group, who searched for evidence of past unacceptable ideas. Generally, the cadres allowed most of the autobiographies of a group to be passed with only token criticism and warnings, but they chose from each group one or two "heavy points" who received concentrated attention. A heavy point endured pressure from his fellow group-members to confess the "real truth" of his past thinking. The suffering of this unfortunate was intended as an object lesson for his companions, who would thus be discouraged from harboring unacceptable ideas. In my discussion group, to my dismay, I found that I was made the heavy point. . . .

No matter what I wrote in my autobiography, my companions rejected it. And with each rejection, the scorn, insults, and threats they heaped on me grew worse. During the day in my office at the mills, I faced much the same from the workers. No one who has never lived day and night as the focal point of such vilification and hatred can understand the effect it has. I could think of nothing but the paper I was having to write and rewrite endlessly. I was long past caring what I confessed to; I only wanted desperately to discover what the Communists expected of me.

At the same time I did not expect to be accused and punished as a counterrevolutionary. In my case, no real evidence of unacceptable thinking existed; moreover, I had given every indication that I supported the regime and endorsed Party policies. I remembered the case of my friend Professor Long, who, during Thought Reform, had broken under pressure and had confessed to crimes of which the authorities later exonerated him; nevertheless, because he had collapsed he had been regarded as being "unable to stand up to the test of political purity." Thus I guessed that I was merely being tested, and my only real fear was that, through some unwitting mistake, I might fail to pass. . . . [For a number of weeks, Loh worked at his regular job during the day and attended his discussion group at night.]

As the weeks passed, . . . I slowly perceived that the period of my stay in the United States interested the cadre the most. Finally, I got on the right track. What was wanted from me mostly was confirmation of the weird picture Communists have of America. I had only to remember the anti-American propaganda and invent personal experiences that made the usual misconceptions seem accurate. Thus I wrote fictional stories of having witnessed horrible scenes in which American police suppressed workers and minority racial groups. I described incidents in which I had suffered unspeakable humiliation. I listed the names and guessed-at addresses of every American I had known, and when the list was not considered long enough I added to it a score of fictitious names and addresses. In every case, these Americans, according to my account, had denounced the Communist Party and had persecuted me because I would not accept their viewpoint. Anyone who read my autobiography would think that I had barely managed to escape from America. I found that the worse I made my picture of the United States, the lighter I could make my own errors in thinking. Ultimately, I needed to say merely that, because of my bourgeois background, some of my own feelings and attitudes had been similar to the American imperialists', and only now did I realize that I had harbored such evil thoughts.

After eight weeks of being struggled against, my autobiography, now 70 pages long, was suddenly accepted as "relatively thorough." The ordeal was over. . . .

The normal relationship between all human beings in China was . . . altered by the Elimination campaign.* Although the campaign turned out to be against only one segment of society, the terror was spread throughout the entire population. It must be understood that the pressure from the

An industrialist and his wife at home. The state purchased his factories and pays 5% interest on the bonds it gave him in exchange. (Photo by Marc Riboud.)

authorities came in a kind of rhythm. Suppression was inflicted, released slightly, and then applied again. Each time the weight descended on us, our apprehension was greater and fear sank deeper. People now were increasingly frightened of each other,

---

* A campaign to eliminate bribery, tax evasion, theft of state assets, cheating in labor and materials, and stealing of state economic information. The campaign was directed particularly at businessmen in preparation for the state purchase of private industry.

and we were so wary of even our closest friends and relatives that free discussion was almost impossible.

I remember the evening when this was brought home to me. I was with the Chans, relaxing in their living room—J.P., Charlie, their wives and me. The children were in bed, and the servants had retired. J.P. happened to mention something about military conscription, and Charlie suddenly said, "What a pity I am over thirty years old and thus do not have a chance to be conscripted as I would wish. I regret that I miss this opportunity to serve my country and my people."

For a moment we were silent as we adjusted to the shock of hearing "group-meeting talk" in a private living room.

Charlie's wife then said quietly, "You are in your house with your family, Charlie. You needn't speak like that to us."

But she was wrong, and we all knew it. I think that each of us was picturing in his mind what would happen if one of us was found unacceptable to the regime. If we were then to save ourselves we would have to denounce him and use our knowledge of him, acquired from years of close friendship, to betray him. Instinctively each of us in that group realized that the others represented the source of his greatest danger. For months, although we outwardly seemed unchanged, our conversation together had been most inconsequential "small talk" interspersed with such "safe" ideas as Charlie had automatically expressed. I know also that when Charlie made his comment each of us experienced a new depth of despair, but we were afraid even to show our anguish. Instead, we returned to the meaningless chatter.

The same night that Charlie made his comment, I began to keep a diary. A lesson I had learned thoroughly from the Elimination campaign was that what we could say with impunity today might be regarded as a capital offense a year later. Many who had been suppressed in the campaign had been heroes not long before. Thus, in my diary, I noted down what I had said during the day in public and in private, and I worked at making all my utterances "correct" and model.

≈§·*Editor's Postscript:* Robert Loh paints a grim picture. No doubt he and people like the Chans suffered considerable anxiety in this period. But it is clear that the Revolution was not intended to serve the interests of men like Loh and Chan. It was, rather, for the people who sweated in Chan's flour and textile mills; it was for the disease-ridden beggars and prostitutes in Shanghai; it was for the poor peasants in Stone Wall Village.

What happened to businessmen like Loh and Chan? The government took over ownership of business and industry and compensated the former owners in bonds, which still pay 5 per cent interest per year. The amount paid a businessman was probably not what he considered his business to be worth, but it enabled him to live better than most Chinese. Former owners often stayed on at their place of business as managers, although their authority now had to be shared with others.

During the weeks in which Loh was writing his autobiography and being criticized, he was going to work every day in a white-collar office job. And Charlie Chan still had servants. Thus it appears that the Communists did not destroy men like these. Instead, they sought, through intense psychological pressure, to win their cooperation in building a new society. Those who were deemed "incorrigible" were sent to the countryside to do physical labor for a period of time, and some, unable to stand the pressure, committed suicide.

There were also some who were executed or jailed. They were those who were convicted, sometimes without much of a trial, of high crimes—big-time gangsters, grain-hoarders, counterrevolutionaries working to bring back Chiang K'ai-shek, opium-pushers, and people who for one reason or another were staunchly anti-Communist. No one seems to know how many were executed. It is doubtful that it was as many as died each year of malnutrition and disease in the old society.

Still, the hardships that resulted for some from revolutionary struggle should not be minimized. Whether or not one favors the Revolution depends in large measure on one's position in the old society. For the peasants of Lin-hsien County, the revolution brought prosperity. For Robert Loh, it brought ruin. ۶≈

Transformation
Building a New Society

Introduction

When the Communists came to power in China in 1949, they faced enormous problems. The country was in chaos after more than a century of warfare with foreign powers and decades of civil strife.

Since the Opium War in 1840, the Chinese had fought five major wars with foreign powers and numerous smaller engagements. The latest foreign war, an eight-year struggle (1937-1945) against the Japanese, had left the country weak and divided.

Agression from abroad had caused or aggravated internal problems in China. The Taiping Rebellion, 1850-1864, had claimed at least twenty million lives, and began a process of rural decay and political disunity that continued for a century. The political structure of traditional China, battered from within and without, collapsed in 1911. There followed decades of armed struggle in which no group was strong enough to eliminate its rivals and reunify the country.

When the Communists finally triumphed and established the Peoples' Republic of China in October, 1949, they faced an immense task. Agricultural production had been disrupted not only by warfare but also by the struggle to redistribute the land which had been the cornerstone of Communist policy during their rise to power. The ubran economy had stagnated under conditions of insecurity and mismanagement. Money had become worthless as policies of the previous Nationalist government under Chiang K'ai-shek led to uncontrolled inflation.

Poverty, ignorance and disease were endemic. Sanitation had broken down and disease was rampant. Malnutrition affected more than half the population. Opium addiction and venereal disease, a legacy of foreign imperialism, were major problems. Illegal secret societies and criminal rackets flourished during the years of political degeneration. The task of reconstruction was complicated for the Communists by the fact that in two decades of struggle with the Nationalists they had never controlled a major city. Suddenly, they had to manage the largest society on earth.

Their early successes were remarkable. By the end of 1952 they had thrown unwanted foreigners out of China for the first time in a century, stopped civil strife, carried out land reform and increased agricultural production to previously unattained levels, ended inflation, reactivated industry and commerce, initiated highly successful campaigns to wipe out epidemic diseases, brought criminal elements under control, and virtually eliminated prostitution, venereal disease and opium addiction. All this was accomplished through a combination of force, persuasion, and the willing cooperation of millions who welcomed the restoration of peace, productivity and national autonomy.

This does not mean the Communists had solved all of China's problems. China specialists often disagree about the effectiveness of various economic measures, or the justice of social reforms, or the ethics of the political system, and so on. And in China itself there had been an intense, sometimes violent, struggle to determine what the future course should be.

Basically, this struggle has involved two groups: those who favor class conflict and those who favor class harmony. Mao Tse-tung, the leader of the first group, believed that China must engage in a continual struggle against the elite classes if it ever hopes to achieve the Communist goal of an egalitarian society. He especially called for constant vigilance and mass criticism of those in authority who were not directly serving the interests of the masses. Moreover, he advocated class discrimination in favor of the peasants and workers rather than the elites who run the country. Only through constant class struggle, Mao felt, could Marx's vision of a classless society be realized.

On the other side are those who favor class harmony, following the lead of Liu-Shao-chi, Chairman of the government of China in 1966, and Teng Hsiao-ping, the preeminent leader in China after Mao's death in 1976. The supporters of the Liu-Teng line criticize Mao's emphasis on class struggle because, they say, it creates chaos, uncertainty and anxiety, making it difficult if not impossible for the leaders to lead. Also, they point out, it discriminates unjustly against the children of the old ruling classes and against the intellectuals who traditionally served as China's ruling elite. The Liu-Teng faction argues that mental workers are also workers, and that all citizens can contribute more effectively to socialism in China if they are free of the constant pressure of class struggle, provided of course that they follow Party guidelines.

Today the Liu-Teng approach holds sway in China, but for almost 30 years Mao's philosophy prevailed. As we have seen in Volume I of *Through Chinese Eyes*, Mao's leadership not only produced a Communist victory but it also led to a social, economic and political revolution that changed almost every aspect of Chinese life: ideology and religion; the status of women and the family; land ownership; and the role of peasants and workers in politics.

Volume II focuses on the struggle to determine policy in China. It begins with a chapter on the Cultural Revolution when differences of opinion clashed head-on. It then examines a number of issues surrounding literature and art, dissent, rural and urban economics, population, pollution, health care and foreign affairs. The volume concludes with a chapter on America as seen through the eyes of Chinese immigrants. We end, then, as we began, with the suggestion that we can learn about ourselves by looking at the world from another perspective.

The Red Guards

⋞§*Editor's Introduction:* The Communist Party has governed China
for many years without permitting any real opposition from other
political parties. But there have been serious disputes within the
Party itself over what policies to adopt. In 1966 disagreements
between two rival factions came to a head. The leader of one group
was Mao Tse-tung, Chairman of the Communist Party. The leader
of the other group was Liu Shao-ch'i, then President of the Government of the People's Republic, and also a high-ranking member
of the Party.

The dispute between them was settled in a major upheaval
known as the Cultural Revolution. Mao was backed by the
army, but he did not use it directly to overthrow his enemies. Instead, he called on the students to shut down the schools and attack
"people in authority" in the Party and government who were "taking
the bourgeois road"—that is, people whose policies tended to favor
the more privileged groups in society, contrary to Mao's "mass line."

The students responded to Mao's call with enthusiasm. They
formed organizations known collectively as the "Red Guards" and,
although they spent most of their time fighting among themselves,
they managed to throw many high officials, including President
Liu Shao-ch'i, out of office. The following account, by a former
Red Guard member—a high school student—indicates the power
the students acquired. It describes the arrest by students of Yeh
Fei, the first secretary of the Fukien Communist Party Committee
and probably the most powerful person in Fukien Province.

Reprinted by permission of G. P. Putnam's Sons from *The Revenge of Heaven*
by Ken Ling. Copyright © 1972 by Dr. Ivan London and Miriam London.

What was wrong with Yeh, according to the Red Guards? What does the discussion of the bathtub indicate about sexual mores in China? &

AT 9 A.M. SHARP on October 24, to the shrill sound of whistles, more than 1,000 fighters assembled in the compound and piled immediately into more than thirty trucks. We arrived at Yeh Fei's residence in less than ten minutes. The contingent from Amoy Eighth Middle was directed to guard the front gate, while those from the other schools were posted to keep a look-out for the security detachment stationed nearby for Yeh Fei's protection.

We knew that this No. 1 personage in Fukien had only five members in his family. His two daughters were away in the north attending universities, and at the moment only an adopted son, an orphan whose father had been a revolutionary martyr, was living at home with Yeh and Wang. The residence occupied a large area, with a fishpond, a little bridge, a flower garden, and a bamboo grove. The walls were topped with a barbed-wire fence.

We rushed directly into the living quarters. . . . Yeh Fei, his wife, Wang Yu-keng, their adopted son, and a little girl we did not know were at the breakfast table, with two servants attending. They must have stopped eating on hearing our footsteps, because they sat there motionless. As we entered the dining room, Yeh Fei's face turned white. He seemed to grasp everything at once and tried to feign composure. He took off his glasses and wiped them without a word.

"Yeh Fei, Wang Yu-keng, stand up! You are under arrest! We are the commandos of the 8-29 Revolutionary Rebellion-Making General Headquarters," Piggy shouted. We had never thought the job could be so easy. . . .

Pushing Yeh and Wang aside, we began our search. We neither handcuffed nor beat them; all we wanted was to seize their authority from them, not to take their lives. In our search we tried our best to keep things intact. We took many photographs to use as evidence. . . .

There were eight rooms in the house; the four upstairs consisted of Yeh and Wang's bedroom with private bathroom, Yeh's study, Wang's study, and the adopted son's room, while downstairs were the living room, dining room, a gymnasium, and the two women servants' quarters. An annex contained a kitchen, a bathroom, and three storage rooms. In the garage there were two black limousines. Outside in the garden there were fruit trees and a badminton court.

We divided the residence into ten areas—the eight rooms plus the storage rooms and surrounding garden—and split ourselves into ten small teams to take thorough inventory. Each item was registered, photographed and assessed in value. We even recorded the reading on the electric meter; the tiniest detail might prove to be revealing and just enough to tip the balance. During the past few months we had seized documents and collected files on Yeh and Wang and interrogated Yeh's close lieutenants, but nothing could be more concrete than what we were doing now.

Those responsible for searching the surroundings measured the total area, the height of the walls, the size of the fishpond, and recorded the number of fish and their probable origin and the kinds of flowers in the garden. They concluded that Yeh and Wang had used their position to build up an unusual collection of fish and plants. They also noted that the space occupied by Yeh and Wang was twenty times that occupied by an average worker. . . .

The first thing that struck us in the living room was the floor, inlaid with an elaborate flower design of different kinds of expensive woods that must have required a lot of people's labor. So we said to Mei-mei, "Imposing hardship on the people and squandering the nation's wealth! Take that down!"

We found more than one hundred bottles of expensive liquor and cigarettes and tea, almost all imported. Wang could not drink because she had high blood pressure. But where did she get all that expensive foreign liquor? When we asked her, she said they were gifts.

"Why did people give these gifts to you and not to me?"

Breastbeater asked. Wang Yu-keng would not answer this question.

We had to record the brands of liquor, cigarettes, and tea, but none of us could read English, so we had to ask Yeh Fei to identify the country of origin on the labels. He obliged smilingly; he knew them all. I stared straight into his eyes and said, "What are you smiling for? How can we have time to study English now when we're devoting ourselves to revolution?"

"I don't know English either. It's just that I'm familiar with the brands."

"You ghoul who sucks the people's blood! Do you know how many days' wages of a worker a bottle of this liquor is worth?" Piggy railed at him.

"These were given to me. I never have been able to make myself drink any because I see the toiling masses working so hard. But it would be a waste to throw them away. So I just keep them there."

We ignored his explanation and ordered him to hold a big batch of foreign liquor and cigarettes while we snapped his picture—to bear the caption "Yeh Fei, the ghoul who sucks the people's blood."

Suddenly, somebody upstairs shouted, "Come up and see how corrupt Yeh Fei and Wang Yu-keng are."

We all dashed upstairs to Yeh and Wang's bedroom. It reeked with fragrance, and in the wardrobe there were expensive cloth, high-heeled shoes, and a big stack of French perfumes. Whoever would have thought this old lady close to fifty was still so coquettish?

What really made us wonder was the size of the tub in the bathroom, larger than any we had ever seen.

"This must be where Yeh Fei and Wang Yu-keng bathe together," someone said.

Whereupon Wang was called in and asked whether this was so. She denied it, saying, "We moved into this house only about two years ago and I was then already well over forty years old. Would I still be disposed to do anything like that?"

A criticism meeting at Peking University. (*From* China Pictorial, *No. 3, 1969, p. 9.*)

"I would worry that Yeh Fei might bring a girl secretary here."

"Oh, no. He leads a very austere life. I trust him."

"Dog fart!"

Someone suggested that we ask Yeh and Wang to try out the tub by bathing together now. Instead, we measured it to see how much wider it was than the usual tub, and although we had no solid proof that Yeh and Wang had indeed bathed in it together, we took pictures of the tub anyway as more evidence of their corrupt mode of life. These data were to appear on big character posters that very day, and the bathtub was to become the major attraction for visitors when the house was opened to the public.

Finally, all of us paid a visit to the storage rooms. They looked almost like an exhibition hall; Yeh and Wang had raked together from all over the country many art objects and scrolls of painting and calligraphy, which they had artistically arranged for display. From our interrogations of Provincial Party Committee cadre members, we had learned that Yeh Fei enjoyed bringing people here to see his collections, after which his subordinates would, of course, know what to present to him to win his pleasure.

We helped the team in charge of these rooms record and assess all the items. Although we all were laymen, we did know that the cost of art objects could not be estimated by their weight. Since there was no time to bring in experts, we marked down figures through sheer guesswork—$300 JMP,* $500 JMP —generally higher than we thought the items were actually worth.

It was past noon when we finished; Yeh Fei and Wang Yu-keng had been on their feet for more than three hours. We concluded with an estimate of the total value of his property and compared it with his salary for the past ten years or so (ten times the wage of a worker). More than ten years before, when he had been first transferred from the military to a provincial post, he had come to Fukien empty-handed. Now he was worth several hundred thousand dollars JMP. More than nine-tenths of his property had come from corrupt activities and exploitation.

Editor's Postscript: This Red Guard report points out a major reason for the Cultural Revolution, as well as some of the methods used. Mao wanted to shake up the Party and government because he feared that after seventeen years in power, many officials had lost their revolutionary ideas and were becoming a new class of bureaucrats, who were serving themselves rather than the people. If Yeh Fei is at all typical, Mao's fears seem to have been well grounded.

As for the Red Guards, Mao worried that the youth of China who had been born after the Communists seized power might not

* JMP, *Jen-min-pi*, Chinese currency. 1 JMP = $.50 U.S.

be good "successors to the revolutionary cause." Mao felt that they should learn revolution by making it. To a great extent, they directed local activities themselves, and they made many mistakes. They made indiscriminate accusations and attacks and frequently used physical force, contrary to Mao's specific instructions. A number of Red Guard units even attacked the military, which for a while stood by helplessly because Chairman Mao had ordered the troops to "support the Left" and not use weapons.

The Red Guards left chaos in their wake. They were inexperienced and so divided among themselves that they could not possibly create new institutions to take the place of the ones that they had destroyed. Eventually the army was commanded to restore order. It then took the lead in establishing "revolutionary committees" to replace the old administrative institutions that had been destroyed by the Red Guards. Gradually, the Party and government were reformed on Maoist lines, and the role of the army in administration declined.

"How I Became a Writer"

❦ *Editor's Introduction:* Literature and art were central concerns of the Cultural Revolution. Indeed, that great upheaval was identified as "cultural" because its main focus was on ideas and the expression of ideas. A *cultural* revolution was needed, Mao reasoned, because although the economic base of society had become socialist—the means of production were owned collectively or by the state—people's thinking lagged behind. Feudal and bourgeois tendencies toward selfishness, individualism and elitism were still prevalent.

The Communists, like their Confucian predecessors, regard literature and art as a powerful tool for shaping thought and action. In his "Yenan Talks on Literature and Art," delivered in 1942, Mao Tse-tung outlined the principles to guide writers and artists in the new society. During the Cultural Revolution Mao's wife, Chian Ch'ing became the principal arbiter of what was artistically acceptable. In her hands, her husband's restrictions on artisitc creativity were even more narrowly defined and rigidly enforced. Her ideas are epitomized in the following essay by a young writer Kao Yu-pao. What principles does he espouse? Do you feel that there is a contradiction between those principles and artistic excellence? Can a revolution be carried out without curbing freedom of expression? ❧

IN THE OLD society I had no chance to go to school. Now the great school of the PLA [People's Liberation Army] provided me with excellent conditions for study. As soon as I knew

Kao Yu-pao, "How I Became a Writer," *Chinese Literature*, No. 6, 1972, pp. 111-17; abridged.

enough characters [written words] I started reading fiction, which thoroughly gripped me, just like the storytellers' tales I loved to hear as a child. Most of the books I read to start with were what we called "old writing," dealing with the emperors, princes, generals, ministers, talented scholars, and beauties of feudal China. Later, on the advice of the leadership, I read new books as well.

One of these raised this thought-provoking question: Why are all the main characters in the old writing members of the ruling classes, with not a single peasant among them? This was the case with the tales I had heard as a child, and with the old novels too. To me, this seemed a very pertinent question. Nobles, officials, and rich landlords had all lived off the sweat and blood of peasants or workers, like my family. Why, then, had no one ever written about *us*, the poor laboring people?

I found the answer to this question later with the help of my comrades by studying the *Yenan Talks*. Chairman Mao points out: "If you are a bourgeois writer or artist, you will eulogize not the proletariat but the bourgeoisie, and if you are a proletarian writer or artist, you will eulogize not the bourgeoisie but the proletariat and working people: it must be one or the other." These words provided the answer to my problem. Like a bright lamp, they lit up the path I should take, laying the ideological foundation for my writing *My Childhood*.

My Childhood is not an autobiography. I wrote it as a novel. According to the *Yenan Talks*, the life reflected in a work of fiction ought to be on a higher plane and more typical than actual everyday life. This involves concentrating the raw material of life and generalizing from it, to make it more typical. But because my first draft was restricted to my personal experience and lacked artistic polish and imagination, my portrayals of both landlord and peasants were superficial.

My comrades advised me to revise this first draft, basing the book mainly on my own experience but using other material as well. In the chapter "The Cock Crows at Midnight," Chou the Old Skinflint mimics the crowing of a cock to rouse his hired hands and make them start work.

Something of this kind happened while I was working for the landlord. Actually, he prodded the cock with a stick to make it crow, but I made him mimic a cock instead, so as to bring out his ruthlessness and craftiness more fully. In this chapter the hired hands discover what the landlord is up to and get their own back by pretending to take him for a thief and beating him up. I heard of such a case when I was small. Incorporating material of this kind made the story more dramatic, the characterization more vivid. In 1955, *My Childhood* was published.

After I had written this book, the Party sent me to middle school and then to university. As I entered the gate of the university, I was stirred by recollections of my childhood. To go to school had been my burning desire. I contrived once to borrow a book, intending to learn a few characters while tending pigs. As soon as the landlord saw that book, however, he seized it and tore it up. [My story] "I Want to Study!" decribes this incident. Now that my dream in the old society had come true in the new, this vivid contrast between past and present spurred me on to study hard for the Revolution.

Apart from my university course, I studied Marxist classics and Chairman Mao's works when I had time. A literary worker who wants to write revolutionary works must first be a revolutionary himself. As our great writer Lu Hsun said:

> To my mind, the fundamental thing for a writer is to be a "revolutionary." If he is, then no matter what he writes about or what material he uses, it will be "revolutionary literature." All that gushes from a fountain is water; all that flows from blood vessels is blood.

To be revolutionaries, we must make a good study of Marxism-Leninism-Mao Tse-Tung thought. This is the major subject which all revolutionaries must study faithfully.

After graduating from university, I went back to the army, in accordance with Chairman Mao's teaching:

> China's revolutionary writers and artists, writers and artists of promise, must go among the masses; they must for a long period of time unreservedly and wholeheartedly go among the masses of workers,

peasants, and soldiers, go into the heat of the struggle, go
to the only source, the broadest and the richest source.

Although I came of a worker-peasant family, I realized
that my thinking and feeling were not quite the same as those
of workers and peasants. Besides, life itself was developing
and changing. New people and things were constantly
coming to the fore. I was familiar with the life of the past. But
to mirror our new age, I must familiarize myself with the new
society and new people, must draw fresh material from life.
The Party branch of our unit backed me up in this, and
arranged for me to go and experience life in villages and
factories . . . .

Life among the masses helped me to remold my thinking.
It supplied me with material for writing, too. One day I went
ploughing with some peasants. During a break for rest they
fell to discussing "The Cock Crows at Midnight," and an old
poor peasant recounted a similar story about a landlord who
roused his cocks at an unearthly hour. In this case, however,
the hired hands banded together to burn down the landlord's
barns and then ran away. This episode held a valuable lesson
for me, deepening my understanding of the revolt of the
proletariat and laboring people against the old social system,
and the nature of their struggle. When I re-read *My
Childhood*, I realized how inadequate was its portrayal of the
nature of different class characters, how limited, shallow, and
inaccurate was its reflection of reality. I made up my mind to
revise the book again.

I rewrote "Solidarity Among the Hired Hands" according
to the account of the old poor peasant. Originally, I had
described how the hired hands' solidarity thwarted the *pao*
[neighborhood] chief's efforts to discover who was responsible for beating up his father, and by way of reprisal he had
them all sent off to do conscript labor. In my altered version, I
laid stress on the courage, resourcefulness, and spirit of revolt
of Kao Yu-pao and the other hired hands. In keeping with this,
I added certain details to bring out more vividly the cruelty of
the negative characters.

I changed the ending of the story too . . . . Originally . . .

Chinese and Western art forms characterize the new culture. This is a shot from a ballet film called "The White-Haired Girl." (From *Chinese Literature*, No. 7, Peking: Foreign Languages Press, 1972, p. 102.)

Kao Yu-pao's family are forced to flee as refugees to Talien, but finally hunger drives them back to their village. That was a thoroughly depressing ending. In the present version Kao Yu-pao, on the advice of some workers, goes to Shantung, where the Party has organized a base of resistance to Japan. The implications of this are more positive, exemplifying the fighting spirit of the laboring people . . . .

Summarizing my development as a writer has brought home to me one truth: Important as is the writer's own experience of struggle, it is only a drop in the ocean compared with the revolutionary practice of the worker-peasant-soldier masses. "The life of the people is always a mine of the raw materials for literature and art . . . . They provide literature and art with an inexhaustible source, their only source." A writer, no matter how talented, if he cuts himself off from the revolutionary struggles of the people, will be unable to write works that they welcome and that give a profound reflection of life. For this reason, literary and art workers must go deep among the masses for long periods of time, taking the road of integration with workers, peasants, and soldiers.

More than twenty years of experience have completely convinced me that Chairman Mao's *Yenan Talks* are like sunlight and dew, nurturing the growth of revolutionary writers and artists. And the revolutionary struggles of the broad masses, our best teachers, are the rich soil in which we grow.

The Disillusionment of Youth

Editor's Introduction: It is probably fair to say that the great majority of students who participated in the Cultural Revolution acted out of idealism. They were convinced that they were in the vanguard of a movement to purge China of corrupt officials and "feudal" ideas and move a step closer to the ideal egalitarian society. When government institutions and the Communist Party itself collapsed as a result of their actions, the People's Liberation Army finally moved in to restore order.

The army had always been the decisive factor in the struggle. Under its commander, Lin Piao, the army had supported Mao's Cultural Revolution, allowing the students free rein for a while. When it took the initiative from the Red Guards, it became the nucleus of "revolutionary committees" formed to replace fallen government institutions. But Lin Piao had ambitious plans of his own. The Chinese now say that in his quest for power, he tried to assassinate Chairman Mao in 1971 and establish a military dictatorship. They report that he was killed when his plane crashed en route to the Soviet Union where he tried to flee after his plot was discovered.

Following Lin's death, Party and government agencies were reestablished, but a ferocious power struggle continued behind the scenes. The faction that was dominant most of the time until Mao's death, in 1976, was led by Mao's wife, Chiang Ch'ing. She and three others, subsequently known as "The Gang of Four," favored the policies of the Cultural Revolution, particularly the vigorous promotion of class struggle. Immediately following Mao's death, they were arrested by Mao's replacement, Hua Kuo-feng, who

Cheng I, "Land and Ocean I Am Grateful to You," *Chinese Youth*, No. 7, 1980. Translated by John Hsu.

accused them of high crimes against the state. At their trial in November, 1980, they were charged with murdering or "persecuting to death" 34,800 people in their quest for power. All four were found guilty. Chiang Ch'ing was given a death sentence, suspended for two years, pending a change of attitude and behavior.

The other faction, led by Teng Hsiao-p'ing, became ascendant after Mao's death and immediately set about reversing most of the policies and programs of the Cultural Revolution. All of China's problems were now blamed on Lin Piao and the Gang of Four, and even Mao was subject to considerable criticism and blame. Lin and the Gang were held responsible for distorting Maoism and making it a religion which no one dared contradict. The new leadership called for demystification of the cult of Mao under the slogan "seek truth from facts," but at the same time, it put its own limits on truth seeking by restricitng the factual data that one could consider. For instance, few would dare to suggest openly that the activities of the Gang of Four were motivated by any but the basest motives.

It is little wonder that these events left many people, particularly young people, cynical about politics and about life in general. The general disillusionment of youth in China has been of great concern to the leadership in the 1980's. Illustrative of the problem is a series of letters on "the meaning of life" published in the journal *Chinese Youth*. The series was initiated by a once idealistic young woman, Pan Hsiao, who had lost all faith in the Communist Party and the Chinese government and had come to view life as a selfish struggle for personal gain. Her letter to the journal was answered by thousands of others expressing both agreement and disagreement with her position. The following selection is from one of those letters. It reads like the collective biography of the youth of the Cultural Revolution generation. The author, contrary to Pan Hsiao, has regained his idealism. On what does he base it? ટ

Dear Comrade Pan Hsiao:

How are you?

I am the author of the short story "Maple." I don't know whether you have read it or not. The story depicts the younger generation's idealism and heroism tinted with modern religious superstition during the Cultural Revolution. It can be said that it epitomizes the spirit of that era. The story is not well-written, but I can guarantee one thing: it is true to life.

This generation of ours spent our early youth in a comparatively stable society. With their exploits, heroes like Lei Feng and other models for young people imbued our crystal-like hearts with the lofty and magnificent idea of "revolution." With great eagerness, we studied Mao Tsetung's Thought and were ready at any time to dedicate all we had to the Chinese revolution and the world revolution.

Comic books have become a popular means of publicizing information and ideas in China. The cartoon illustrates Mao's assertion that: "The day the women of the whole country arise is when the Chinese revolution will be victorious." The young woman in the picture is suggesting to her Party Secretary that a women's militia unit be established during the Chinese Civil War.

When the Cultural Revolution got underway, our revolutionary enthusiasm erupted like a volcano. Swimming with the tide and obeying the orders of the proletarian headquarters, we plunged into the whirlpool of struggle. Finally, however, history mercilessly displayed before us the harsh reality. In the face of these bloody facts, all the lies and deceptions became obvious one after another. The myth about the sanctity of Mao Tse-tung's Thought exploded, and so did the deity himself. Ideas, life, hope, and courage were all ruined.

I had been most eager to pitch into the struggle. Being concerned about the nation's destiny, I ran across several provinces and municipalities, joining the youthful forces of the Cultural Revolution. But I saw the killing of more than 2,700 people in the so-called struggle by violence in a small prefecture called Luzhou. In addition dozens of boats and ships were sunk or destroyed. Could this have been done for the sake of "revolution" as conceived by the people?

Like you, we were seized by all kinds of anxiety and misgivings. But as we studied Chairman Mao's exhortations to "combat selfishness and criticize revisionism," we piously criticized our hesitation and wavering as simply a manifestation of a *petit bourgeois* mentality. Therefore as soon as we young people were called upon to resettle in the countryside, we all eagerly signed up without any reluctance. Everyone was determined to integrate himself with the worker and peasant masses and to reform the "deep-rooted bad habits of the *petit bourgeoisie* " by doing arduous labor.

Among my schoolmates who went to Taigu County, Shansi Province, some had deformed legs, some had chronic diseases, and others were under the age requirement for living and working in the countryside. They had applied many times before they were approved. Some even wrote application letters with their blood. A batch of us, some thirty in number, were assigned to a commune named Pingchuan. We did not accept the assignment, but went to see the leader in charge, asking her to send us to a commune where conditions were the most difficult. At first, she mistook our request as an expression of dislike for the commune to which we were assigned. She explained to us again and again that the commune was not bad and one could get high bonuses there. When she finally understood our intention, she was so moved that for a while she was unable to utter a word.

In this way we came to a mountainous commune in the remotest part of Taigu County, the only commune that did not have electricity. As soon as we put down our luggage, we went through the village, visiting the poor peasants and presenting to every household Chairman Mao badges and his works. Braving the coldest weather in a year in that highland, we took up our hoes early the next morning to dig up the earth and fill the gullies in order to reclaim land for agriculture. Thus, in a little mountainous village of only nine families located in the chain of Taihang mountains, we started our difficult life as rusticated youths with high spirit and vigor.

My friends and I were deeply grateful for being resettled in the countryside. It brought us from the dazzling blue sky of idealism down to the cold and harsh earth of reality. Rustication opened our eyes for the first time to the real countryside in China not to be found in propaganda, and to the peasants' real feelings of joy, anger, sorrow and happiness.

With the courage of being ready to gulp down all the sufferings of the world at once, we pitched into the struggle to remake nature. On the first day alone I broke several hoe handles while digging with all my might. At the risk of my life, I used a wire only ten meters long as a detonating cord for dynamiting rocks. In spite of the production team leader's dissuasion, another schoolmate and I jumped into the mountain torrents to salvage timber owned by the collective. Some schoolmates experimented in growing rice in the mountainous region despite the difficulties. Even our girl schoolmates carried on their shoulders rocks and manure buckets, and so did the schoolmates with deformed legs. Instances like this are too many to enumerate.

Nevertheless, our blood and sweat were of little avail. Our ideal of building a socialist new countryside suffered severe setbacks under the "left" deviationist line which called for "evaluating one's work according to political performance" and "conducting agricultural production by exercising proletarian dictatorship."

Resettlement also helped us to sober down for the first time and reflect on the Chinese Revolution. When looking at Peking from afar, we were pained to find that the end result of the Cultural Revolution was not a much better society as had been promised. The so-called "capitalist roaders" were toppled, but in their place emerged a feudal, fascist dictatorship we had never seen before. Lin Piao's attempted coup especially shocked us like a thunderbolt. Any apology or excuse could in no way cover up the lightning that made our souls tremble. We were faced with a deep spiritual crisis!

Some schoolmates were unable to stand a life of deception and loss of faith. They committed suicide as a protest, though a thin voice it was against society. Some sank into degradation, engulfed in the turbid waves of life. However, there were still quite a few comrades who started thinking things out on their own; they were searching for answers from the realities of society and Marx's works. We did physical labor in the daytime and conducted extensive and in-depth social surveys. At night we read and studied. For a period of time, we had only one kerosene lamp and had to make do by reading in three shifts. Some read while others went to sleep. In the dimly-lit cave, we took turns studying until daybreak.

I had been the most pious and therefore was also the most disappointed. Confronted with harsh realities, my girl friend nearly committed suicide, and I went to the north of the Shanhai Pass and roamed about in the forests of the Xing-an Mountains and in the prairies of Hulunbeier. I took up odd jobs and did hard labor. I carried with me a set of carpentry tools and wrapped myself in a worn-out dog hide. My satchel was filled with works by Marx, Feuerbach and Huxley. I wanted to see the world, I wanted to find out from my 3,000-mile journey and from the sweat and toil I spent in dozens of towns and villages something true and reliable.

Some of my friends wrote economics essays to criticize theories advocated by Lin Piao and the "Gang of Four" concerning the basic economic law of socialist society, and because of this they were placed under surveillance for quite a few years. Still others took up the pen, broke through literary blockades, and produced a number of poems and articles opposing Lin Piao and the "Gang of Four." These hand-copied manuscripts soon got around and became "underground literature" of considerable influence at that time. In this way the old religion fell apart like an avalanche, while a new faith was still in the difficult process of being conceived.

There has never been a generation, I dare say, that has

experienced such terrible spiritual collapse and mental torture as we have. Our revolutionary predecessors, once they discovered the truth of revolution, threw themselves into the people's cause, courageously and faithfully carrying on the struggle. They did not have the pain of wavering and losing faith that we have experienced. To whom could we turn? The "Gang of Four," by stealing the name of the leader and the Party, had everything under their control and monopolized the right to interpret Marxism-Leninism and Mao Tse-tung's Thought. In the darkness we could only explore Marxist theories on our own, groping forward in a painful mood of negating the past.

We are grateful to the vast expanse of life in society. At the bottom of society we experienced an acute and complex struggle marked with the characteristics of the new era. We were maturing, embracing again the great truth of Marxism. We are now espousing a Marxism that is no longer superstition shrouded in the halo of myth, nor the means and tool which certain conspiratorial cliques employed to exercise an "all-round dictatorship" over the people in order to strengthen their rule of feudal fascism. It is a scientific world outlook, the truth for the emancipation of all mankind! We are grateful to the deep ocean of the people! They are like a mother to us and it is in their arms we have healed our wounds, returned to life and drawn courage and strength.

This is the history of how we changed from a generation of blind and pious faith to a generation of tenacious thinking. Some older comrades understand this, but some news media and leadership just make endless accusations against us. I have no intention of defending our conduct; rather, I only want to make a relatively objective review of history. True, there are hoodlums, thieves and murderers among us. But whenever I call to mind this generation of ours, first to appear before my eyes are a group of kind and generous laborers. I cannot go against my conscience and show disappointment in them. This is because I understand them. I know for sure they hate evil like an enemy, and behind their sometimes extremist language is a child's innocent heart beating for the motherland, the people and the Party.

"A Newcomer," painting in the traditional style by Yang Chih-kuang. (From *Chinese Literature*, No. 3, Peking: Foreign Languages Press, 1972, p. 48.)

Just as every generation has its own merits and shortcomings, we, too, have many drawbacks and problems. For example, we lack a sense of duty, a sense of being the masters of the country. We are not constructive in nature and are short of cultural cultivation. We have done more destruction than construction, and we are skeptical about more things than we affirm. But if we analyse the matter in a materialist perspective and assume that all this came as a result of a social life which had been turned upside down, then after having smashed the "Gang of Four," we have reason to believe that in a stable and united social environment all these problems can be solved step by step under positive guidance.

Comrade little Pan, it is my feeling that you have not truly seen through life. For thousands of years humans have tenaciously searched for the value of existence; they seek the truth of life, pursuing the true, the good and the beautiful. You are only 23 years of age and your experience cannot be regarded as profound and mature. It is inappropriate for you to blurt out that you "see through" everything. Your understanding at this stage is only one phase of your life. You will not stop at this point and your path is by no means narrowing. Precisely because you are persistently exploring and are not fearful of hardships, you are standing at the threshold of truth. It is possible for you to find a valuable life and thus become a most enthusiastic and valiant fighter. Of course we cannot rule out the other possibility. Don't hide yourself in love, and don't evade the crisis of your faith, but move forward to meet it head-on. Your age is the best time to solve the problem of your outlook on life. If you turn from it, you will achieve nothing in your whole life. If you step up to it and find a good solution, you will sweep forward irresistibly like water pouring from a steep roof.

The Paupers' Co-op

Editor's Introduction: Agriculture affects almost everything in China: nutrition, health, industry, foreign trade and politics. The debates over literature and art, as important as they were to the Cultural Revolution, were nowhere as important, ultimately, as the debates over agricultural policy.

Eighty percent of China's one billion people live in the countryside. As we have seen in Volume I, the revolution overthrew the traditional landlord system and redistributed the land to the peasants. Unfortunately, land reform did not solve the economic problems in the rural areas. Farmers were given small, inefficient plots of land to work, and most of them had no recourse but to sell their new land and become tenants again. The alternative was to move to overcrowded cities where jobs were scarce or nonexistent.

The Communists' solution to this dilemma was to form collective farms. The goal was to create larger, more efficient farms and thus encourage peasants to stay in the rural areas. The following selection, "The Paupers' Co-op," is a fictionalized account of how a farming cooperative got started in one area. It describes the benefits of cooperative effort and the obstacles that must be overcome to attain it.

As you read "The Pauper's Co-op" bear in mind that stories of this sort—sometimes called "new socialist literature"—were

Tang Keng-liang, *The Paupers' Co-op* (Peking: Foreign Languages Press, 1965), abridged.

originally written not for us but for the Chinese. The purpose of such stories is to teach a lesson or provide a model of good conduct. What values are being promoted by this story? What is the role of the Communist Party? What are its methods? 🮲

IN A CERTAIN county of Hopei stands a mountain called Ch'ang-yu, and in the valley below lies Ch'ang-yu Village, a village always known for its poverty: poor hills, poor water, poor soil, and poor people, too. . . .

The village had 154 households, but three out of four consisted of poor peasants or hired hands, of whom several dozen had to beg for a living.

Soon after Liberation came land reform, when the poor and lower-middle peasants were given some land of their own. But lack of tools, draft animals, fertilizer, and funds made it impossible to grow good crops or to cope with drought and flood. Some of the former poor peasants and hired hands found themselves having to sell their newly won land.

The few [Communist] Party members in the village cudgelled their brains day and night to think of some way out. One of these, Wang Ku-hsing, was a big, burly man and a good farmer. He foresaw that the 1952 crop failure would make it hard for the villagers to last through the winter; and it would be a disgrace if they had to apply to the state again for relief. . . .

Wang went to see District Party Secretary Tsao. He was back the next morning and told Tu Hung, "Good news!"

"What good news?"

"The district cadres are examining some directives on agricultural cooperation. They want to have another try at setting up a few co-ops. Secretary Tsao said, 'So long as we poor stand together and follow Chairman Mao's line on agricultural cooperation, we can join forces in co-ops. If we pull together we can make the earth produce gold. Step by step we'll shake off our poverty.'"

"Very good," cried Tu. "I've been wishing we could have a co-op ever since I heard that other districts were trying them. We must make a go of it."

Wang called together all the Party members to pass on Secretary Tsao's advice. Then they went off to try to persuade the villagers to form a cooperative.

This wasn't easy. Why not? Because co-ops were something new. No one had any idea what they were like or what their advantages were. So most of the peasants had doubts.

Some said, "If so many people are thrown together there are bound to be quarrels and fights, even families breaking up."

"Several dozen households farming together? They'll never agree. Everything will be messed up."

"Too many cooks spoil the broth. Too many sons means none support their father. We're better off without co-ops."

But the Party members didn't lost heart. They went on canvassing. And finally twenty-three households agreed to take the cooperative road proposed by the Party.

"Good," said Wang. "We'll start with twenty-three households. If we make a go of it, others will want to join."

A meeting was held to set up the co-op. The twenty-three families who went saw at once that they were all poor peasants, the poorest in the whole village. This really was a Paupers' Co-op. They elected Wang as chairman and Tu as vice-chairman.

When they reckoned up their assets, the co-op owned nearly forty acres of land, but no draft animals at all except for three legs of a donkey. Three legs of a donkey? Well, this donkey was the joint property of five households. Four of them had joined the co-op, but not the fifth; so one leg of the donkey didn't belong to the co-op. That meant they had a three-quarter share in this donkey. And not having a single ox or cart, how were they to till the land? . . .

"Of course, we've got hands," said Li. "But where's the money for animals and carts to come from?"

Wang pointed out of the window. "There! Animals, carts, tools—we'll get the lot up there!"

All eyes turned to the mountains ten miles away. They couldn't for the life of them see how they were to provide animals and carts.

"The mountain's covered with brushwood, isn't it?" Wang continued. "Cut some and sell it, and we'll be able to buy all we need.". . .

In twenty days they cut more than twenty tons of brush-wood, which they sold in town for 430 *yuan*. Was everyone pleased! These paupers had never handled so much money. . . . Instead of sharing out the money, they went to town and bought an ox, a mule, a cart, and nineteen sheep. The whole co-op exulted over the purchases. . . .

[W]illing as the paupers were to work, they were still hard

The fruits of collective labor—water conservation, erosion control, and increased crop land. (From *China Reconstructs*, January, 1973, p. 9.)

up, and long before harvest time they ran out of grain. Some cooked a whole basket of greens with a handful of rice; others had nothing at all to put in the pan. When Tai Ming collapsed in the fields from hunger, Wang took him home and made him a broth of the last few beans in their house. He and his wife now had to make do with wild plants.

Hunger affected the co-op members' work and their morale, too.

Li Ying started grousing in the fields, "If I hadn't joined the co-op," he said, "I could have sent my son out as a hired hand. That way I'd have had one less mouth to feed and some cash at the end of the year. Now we haven't so much as a grain of rice, yet he expects us to feed him."

Li Ying's boundary stones were in the way of the plough, and one co-op member started to move them away. But Li growled, "Don't waste your time shifting those. After the autumn harvest I'm leaving the co-op. I'd only have to lug them back again."

Later someone urged Wang, "Let's pick some of our unripe crop, Old Wang, just enough to keep us from starving!"

"And spoil our harvest? No!" said Wang. "We must tighten our belts now to reap more grain later on. We'll find some other way out."

The Party members talked it over and solved the problem again the poor man's way. They could cut brambles, strip the leaves off for compost, and sell the stems to buy grain. . . .

The Party had taken an interest in this new co-op from the start. When the district Party secretary learned of its predicament, he hurried to Ch'ang-yu Village with a loan.

"Don't worry about us, we're all right," said Wang. "I guarantee no one will die of hunger!"

"All right, are you?" retorted Tsao. "You're as pale as a ghost, man!"

Wang covered his face with his hands and laughed. "That's my natural color. I'm not hungry."

"Not hungry? You haven't eaten a grain of rice for days."

"I don't mind missing a few meals if the co-op can grow strong enough so that none of our members need ever go hungry again. Besides, the Party and the government have much bigger problems to cope with. We don't want to add to their burden."

With Party members like these, who always put others

Collective harvest. (From *Jen-min hua-pao,* 1971, Nos. 7–8, pp. 20–21).

first and work so whole-heartedly for the common good,
thought Secretary Tsao, they're bound to make a success of the
co-op. "Comrade," he said, "if people have problems, it's up to
the state to help. Buy some grain with this fifty *yuan,* and go
on finding ways to tide yourselves over. If you succeed, cooperation will take root in this poor mountain valley. And that
will be wonderful."

They bought grain for the co-op with the loan. Deeply
touched, one member fingered the grain and declared, "They
say that nobody is as dear as a mother. But the Party cares for
us better than a mother. Just in the nick of time the Party's
sent us this loan to see us through."

The co-op's maize grew tall and strong. By harvest time
each cob was about a foot long, as plump as a pestle, and cov-

ered with symmetrical golden kernels the size of horses' teeth.
. . .

Now the harvest was shared out. Li Ying's family of seven
owned two acres of land and three of its members worked. The
previous year in the mutual-aid team they had harvested six
piculs of grain; this year in the co-op they got forty-one. Li
Ying jumped for joy and caught Wang by the arm. "Let's move
those boundary stones away, chairman," he cried. "They use
up a furrow or two of land, and get in our way as well."

"Don't let's tire ourselves out shifting those," chuckled
Wang. "We'll only have to help you lug them back in a few
days."

"Come off it, chairman! My mind's made up. I'm in the
co-op for life. You couldn't get me to leave even if you kicked
me out."

It had been a tough year, but already the paupers' co-op
had shown the advantages of cooperation. After the harvest,
sixty new families joined, bringing the total to eighty-three
households. Hard work and thrifty management enabled the
co-op to forge ahead every year, so that by 1956, three years
later, Ch'ang-yu Village had changed out of all recognition.
Every household entitled to had joined the co-op, and now
they combined with three neighboring villages to form a cooperative of the more advanced type. By now their poor mountain valley had grown rich, the barren hills were smiling; flinty
tracks had been transformed into smooth highways, thatched
huts into tiled stone houses; and every single family had surplus grain and money in the bank. . . .

Things got better year by year in Ch'ang-yu Village. In
1958, several co-ops merged in the Kuang-ming People's Commune, with Wang as its chairman. Now it is 1962, just ten
years after the co-op was set up. What earth-shaking changes
these brief ten years have seen! In 1952, they started a co-op
with a three-quarters' share in a donkey. Today they've gone a
long way toward mechanizing agriculture. They have tractors
to plough the fields, electric pumps, motors to hull rice, trucks
to transport their produce.

Ten years ago there was more sand than soil on the stony hills, so that the crops were spoiled by flood or drought. In these ten years, they've built reservoirs and canals, changing the sandy hillsides into irrigated fields; they can water the crops in time of drought, and pump out excess water in time of flood. In place of six hundredweight an acre, they now raise one and a half tons or so, and the once barren hills are covered with fruit trees. So Ch'ang-yu Village today has rich mountains, rich water, rich soil, and rich people, too.

Six families out of ten have built new houses. . . .

If you stand on a hill in the evening and look down, the electric lights are like pearls gleaming in the dark, and Ch'ang-yu Village is a beautiful sight!

Changes in the Rural Economy

≈ξ Editor's Introduction: Near the end of *The Pauper's Co-op* the merging of small cooperatives into larger communes is described. The communes, which range in size from about 10,000 people to 75,000 people, are large enough to mobilize labor for big projects such as land reclamation, water conservation, irrigation, road construction and so on, and to accumulate capital for schools, medical clinics and small factories.

The Communes are divided into "brigades" and "work teams" averaging about 2,000 and 200 people respectively. In most communes, the work teams are the "basic accounting unit," that is, team members are collectively responsible for investment in production and for distribution of income when crops are harvested. The land is owned collectively by the people who live on it, and not by individuals or the state, though there are a few state farms.

Most families own their own homes, and each household has a private plot on which it can raise food and animals for its own use or for sale at market. A farm worker's income depends on how much his team produces, how much effort he has put into that production (measured in work points), and how much he raises on his private plot. A family might also receive some money on the basis of need. Some teams are wealthier than others because they have better land or because they farm more effectively.

When a team harvests its crop, it distributes some of it among the team members and sells the rest to the state for distribution. Some of the money derived from sales to the state goes to various levels of the collective for such things as schools, hospitals,

He Jianzhang, "Present Economic Policies, What and Why?", *China Reconstructs,* January 1981, pp. 4-6.

administration and investment in new production (seeds, tools, irrigation pumps, etc.), and some is divided among individuals.

Collectivization has been effective for distributing wealth much more evenly than before, and that is no small accomplishment. But there is considerable dispute in China and by analysts outside China about whether collective farming is the most effective method of production. They point to small family farms in Japan, for instance, which produce more food per unit of land than do collective farms in China. But Japanese agriculture depends on heavy inputs of fertilizer, insecticides and irrigation which require a lot of money. The Chinese do not have the money to spend, but they do have a lot of people, and they can work more effectively together than individually, it is argued. The Chinese have decided to stick with their "socialist path" but one with several twists and turns.

The following article, written in 1981 by the deputy director of the Institute of Economics in the State Planning Commission of China, criticizes some of the agricultural decisions made during the Cultural Revolution. What problems does the author see in Chinese agriculture? What solutions does he offer? How does the life of a Chinese farmer differ from that of an American farmer? ह्

ABOUT 80 PERCENT of China's population is rural. Agriculture provides practically all of her foodstuffs and 70 percent of the raw materials for her light industry. Farm and livestock products make up a quarter of her exports. So what happens in agriculture is important to the people's life, and to political stability, industrial growth and foreign trade. In the readjustment now being made in the entire national economy, therefore, that of rural policies is primary.

Since the founding of the new China, her agricultural production has steadily increased, stimulated first by the land reform, then by the collectivization and technical transformation of agriculture. Grain output rose from 113.2 million tons in 1949 to 304.75 million tons in 1978. That of cotton increased from 445,000 tons to 2,167,000 tons in the same period. But the productivity of agricultural labor is still low. Alongside some mechanization and semi-mechanization, most farm work is still manual. This fairly undeveloped and uneven situation requires a policy which allows various economic forms and ways of management to exist and grow in the countryside—

always provided socialist public ownership holds the dominant place.

The Problems

From long before the "cultural revolution," however, China's policies on agriculture were divorced from the real level of development of her productive forces. The idea was: the bigger the collective unit and the higher the level of public ownership, the better. So too much stress was placed on the transition from smaller to larger-scale collective ownership; some places even rushed on to public (state) ownership before the conditions were ripe. Calls were issued to restrict and even eliminate the individual economy. In farm management, the principle of adapting to local conditions was overlooked; instead all rural communes and brigades were urged to learn from a single model. Result: China's rural economy lost diversity and vitality.

Spreading "night soil" as fertilizer in Yangtze valley.(Photo by Richard Bartlett)

During the "cultural revolution" things got worse under the pernicious influence of the gang of four. The label "capitalist" was applied to most of the diversified activities of the people's communes (which include farming, forestry, animal husbandry, fish-breeding, etc.). In particular it was slapped on the sideline occupations of peasant households, on their small plots for personal use and on trade at village fairs—which were restricted or banned. Also violated were sound systems of labor management, and the principle of "to each according to his work." On the pretext of repudiating material incentives, the gang asserted that all should be treated alike, the diligent and the idle, the skilled and the unskilled. They were against work quotas, appraisal of work and allotment of work points. Thus they blocked the initiative of the collective economic units and of the peasants as individuals. As a result the development of agriculture was slowed down.

The Remedies

To remedy this situation, policies for readjustment have been adopted as follows:

First, the size of the production teams is to vary as local conditions require. Besides the state farms, there are now 90,000 people's communes in China's countryside. These are managed on three different levels: commune, production brigade and production team. The production team is, as a rule, the basic accounting unit. Teams which are too big (i.e. consist of more than 20-30 families), or those whose members are widely spread so that these teams lag in production because of difficulties in organizing work can be split up into smaller ones. In communes where the basic accounting unit has been prematurely raised to the brigade level (as often happened under the influence of the ultra-Leftist line) it is necessary to change it back to the team—if production hasn't benefited and members feel dissatisfied.

Secondly, more flexible and diverse forms of management and of responsibility for production are required within the teams in accord with their conditions (level of production, standard of living, crop characteristics of different localities). Collective production is to be geared more closely to the

A procession of carts and animals along a rural road in Northern China.(Photo by Peter Seybolt)

personal benefit of commune members. In some cases, year-round small work groups, responsible for particular jobs and with pay according to output, can be formed under the teams. Temporary or seasonal groups with limited responsibility can also be organized. Groups, or households, can specialize in occupations requiring more technique such as poultry-raising, gardening or fish-breeding. In some poor teams, where the population is scattered and production low, responsibility for work can be brought down to the households.

Thirdly, plots, livestock, trees and mountain slopes for private use that have been curtailed or abolished are to be restored and household sideline production and trade at local fairs developed.

Fourthly, production teams will no longer be restricted from processing farm and sideline products and doing trade.

Teams are encouraged to progress toward an integration of farming, handicrafts and commerce.

Fifthly, in the collective sector, the rights of management and decision-making of rural communes and production teams will be respected. The state will issue no more orders on their cultivation plans. It will only put forward quotas for a few major products (including grain, cotton and oilseeds) that communes, brigades and teams should sell to the state. And the state purchases will themselves gradually shift from a mandatory quota basis to a contract basis. Teams are to decide for themselves what crops they will grow, what land they will use for them, methods of cultivation, disposition of their surplus products and distribution of income. There will be no administrative intervention in such affairs by any level of government.

Sixth, the purchase prices of farm products will be raised substantially. Last year, the state added appropriations of over 10 billion yuan* for this purpose. In the future, on the basis of more production and greater revenues, the state will allot more funds each year to further raise the prices paid to products of farm and sideline and for adjusting the price ratios between industrial and agricultural products, and between different farm products.

Some Results

These new policies have won a warm and universal welcome from China's peasants, bringing new vitality to the rural economy. Agricultural growth, slow in the past, is accelerating. Increases in grain production in 1978 and 1979 exceeded 49 million tons: the biggest increase for any two consecutive years since the founding of the People's Republic. Production of oilseeds, meat and industrial crops has risen. The peasants' income from the collective economy grew considerably in 1979, to a national average of 83.4 yuan per capita. This, plus income from family sidelines, has improved their livelihood.

* One yuan equals $1.50.

The Iron Man of Taching

◄§ Editor's Introduction: Industrial development in China, like agricultural development, has relied heavily on labor power. Economists characterize much of China's production as "labor intensive" rather than "capital intensive." In a labor intensive economy humans do much of the work done by machines in a capital intensive economy such as that of the United States. In China, workers have been exhorted to be self-reliant and self-sufficient, to work hard and overcome all problems through their own efforts. Workers who best exemplify those traits are rewarded and held up as models to inspire others. One such model is "Iron Man Wang," a worker at the Taching oil fields.

The following story was written during the Cultural Revolution. Note the constant comparison between industrial production and making war. What virtues should a good worker and a good soldier have in common according to the author? §►

was not a simple drilling operation but a declaration of war against imperialism, revisionism, and the whole old world.

There followed five days and nights of strenuous work. Then glistening jet-black crude oil—the first Taching oil—came gushing out of the well! The huge oilfield, sealed for thousands of years, began yielding up its treasures. Wang Chin-hsi and his team gathered round, beside themselves with joy at the sight of that spurting column. "Long live Chairman Mao!" they cheered. "Long live Chairman Mao!"

It was not all plain sailing from then on, however. Soon after this first well was drilled an accident happened.

At dawn on May Day, under Wang Chin-hsi's supervision, they started dismantling the derrick to "move house." Both arms raised, his eyes on the drill, Wang moved back step by step, shouting directions.

Then, without warning, a drill pipe hurtled down. The team leader, struck on the legs, was knocked unconscious.

When Wang Chin-hsi came to, he saw that the derrick was not yet dismantled but that the political instructor and his comrades had stopped work to gather round and revive him.

"I'm not a clay figure, so easily smashed," Wang protested. With a great effort, he stood up. As he did so, blood soaked through his trouser legs, staining his shoes and socks.

The political instructor tore a strip from his own overalls to bandage the team leader's wound. With amazing tenacity, Wang, both arms raised high, went on directing the work.

Wang's legs became so badly swollen that his mates insisted he go to the hospital. But he would not hear of this. "Norman Bethune came all the way to China to help our revolution, and gave his life here. What's a leg wound?" he said. He told them on no account to spread word of his injury or report it to those in charge.

Wang's comrades, unable to persuade him to leave his fighting post or rest, made him pair of crutches. But whenever any of the leading comrades arrived he would hide these crutches in a pile of pipes and stand up unaided to report on the work and ask for new assignments.

Before long, however, those in charge learned what had happened and packed Wang off to the hospital.

Even when lying in bed in the hospital, Wang's heart was in the oilfield. In his mind's eye he saw his mates, strong and active as tigers. This was no time for him to be lying there, while the others battled for oil.

The next day another patient was brought in by truck. Wang seized his chance, when no nurses were about, to limp out on his crutches and clamber onto the truck, which took him back to his post.

To build the oilfield fast and well, Wang Chin-hsi and his comrades battled round the clock. But his legs grew more swollen from day to day, until finally the leadership, backed by his teammates, sent him to a hospital farther away from Taching. They urged the medical staff there to keep a strict eye on him, and he was put in the charge of a young doctor.

To be unable to work is the greatest hardship for a man of Wang's calibre. One hand on his bedside table, the other on a crutch, he propped himself up. Beads of sweat stood out on his forehead.

"My mates are going all out to build the oilfield," he informed the doctor. "How can I lie here idle?"

"You're in no condition to work," rejoined the other. "We're responsible for getting you back into shape."

"It's a serious matter, our country's lack of oil. This scratch on my leg is nothing. Can a few bumps and bruises stop making revolution?" Wang rose painfully to his feet.

"The leadership has entrusted you to my care. This is my fighting post, my job."

"My fighting post is at the oilfield, doctor." Gazing at the young doctor, Wang spoke with feeling. "My job is drilling oil wells for our country. Won't you help me get back to my post, where my duty lies?"

The young doctor, stirred by Wang's revolutionary spirit, went off to consult his leadership. Too impatient to wait for his return, Wang slapped on his cap and stumped out of the ward on his crutches, taking the next train back to the scene of battle. It was dark and pouring with rain when he reached Taching. Too dark to distinguish mud, water, earth, or sky, he slithered along as best he could through the night.

At 1 AM, knocking on the door woke the men of Team 1205. When they lit a lamp and opened the door, they discovered this runaway patient from the hospital, leaning on a crutch. His injured leg was in a plaster cast. He was soaked to the skin and all over mud from his head to his bandaged feet. They hurriedly made up his bed. But by the time they looked round to urge him to rest, Wang had slipped out again behind their backs and limped on his crutches to the oil well.

Some time later, Wang Chin-hsi and his men were seated on some pipes discussing their work when—Wham! The heavy cement lid weighing several dozen pounds was blasted off the top of the drilling machine. A blowout was imminent.

A blowout is the most serious accident that can happen in an oilfield. When the mud specific gravity is too low, the oil and gas in a well burst through the earth to erupt like a volcano, striking sparks from the hurtling stones. The whole oilfield may turn into a sea of flame. A huge towering derrick may sink into the well. Wang held a hasty council of war with his mates and reported what had happened to headquarters.

The usual way of preventing a blowout is to increase the mud specific gravity with heavy spar. But in this newly opened oilfield, where the wells were still few and far between, heavy spar . . . would have to be fetched from far away. It would come too late to avert an accident. With great presence of mind, Wang came to a swift decision: They would pour cement into the mud tank.

This method had never been used before. It meant risking getting the drill stuck in the well. But Wang knew from previous investigations that the water here was too alkaline for the cement to harden immediately. If they took steps quickly to avert a blowout, there would still be time to deal with the cement.

"Pour in cement!" he ordered.

The whole team went into action. It was a tense battle.

Sack after sack of cement and loads of earth were poured into the sump.

A mixer was needed to mix the cement with the mud, but they had none at hand. Wang tried stirring the cement with a crutch, but this proved ineffective. Throwing away his crutches then, he jumped into the waist-deep mud.

Completely oblivious to his own pain, Wang trampled and stirred the mixture with hands and feet, moving swiftly and vigorously. The cement kept sinking to the bottom of the tank. As he stooped to stir it, mud bespattered his face. But simply tossing his head, he went on mixing.

Some young fellows quickly followed his example.

After a battle lasting over three hours they got the blow-out under control, saving the oil well and the drilling machine.

Iron Man Wang Chin-hsi (on the right) with fellow workers. (From Jen-min hua-pao, 1971, No. 9.)

By that time, the highly alkaline mud had raised great blisters on their hands. And when his mates helped Wang out of the tank, his legs were so painful that he could no longer stand. Drops of sweat coursed down his face. Nonetheless, he squared his shoulders, reached for his crutches, and struggled to his feet.

"Never mind about me," he ordered. "Go on drilling."

Shortly before this, Aunt Chao had arrived from Ma-chia-yao with a basket of hard-boiled eggs. Tears in her eyes, she gazed at the drill-team leader. His sunken eyes were bloodshot. His prominent cheekbones stood out more sharply than ever. His short beard was caked with mud. Yet he stood his ground on the high drilling platform like some intrepid warrior, his muddy figure transformed by the golden sunlight into a splendid statute of glinting bronze. . . .

In all her sixty-odd years, Aunt Chao had never set eyes on such a sight. With lips that trembled she declared: "Team Leader Wang, you're a real man of iron!"

That is how the name "Iron Man" spread through Taching.

Editor's Postscript:

By publicizing the deeds of model workers, such as Iron Man Wang, the Government of China hoped to encourage people to work hard and produce more. Reward would come in the form of praise, publicity, and an increase in collective well-being.

In a capitalist economy encouragement for hard work and increased production usually takes a more material form — for example, increased wages, profits or bonuses. Such material rewards were denounced in China during the cultural revolution as symptomatic of a capitalist mentality. People were encouraged to work selflessly for the good of all, and not for immediate personal gain.

Since the end of the Cultural Revolution that policy, like so many others, has been changed. Model workers such as Wang are still publicized, but individual material rewards have become the principal means to encourage workers. Exhortation and collective rewards are now considered too abstract to elicit the desired response from workers.

Likewise, there have been other changes in economic practice since the Cultural Revolution. Use of the market system to help regulate production and prices is an important case in point.

In a capitalist economy most decisions about what is to be produced, and what the price of a product will be, are determined by the market, that is, by consumer choice. Prices vary according to supply and demand.

In a socialist economy some production and price decisions are determined by the market, but many are made by the government. The government might decide, for instance, that the limited resources of a nation should be invested in increasing food production or in housing for the poor. In a market economy, those resources might be invested in the production of luxury apartments or expensive automobiles for the rich because there is a demand for those products by those who have money.

In many third world countries, that is exactly what happens. Production is heavily weighted toward production for the rich or production of goods for sale abroad. In either case, poor people, who are the majority of the population in most third world countries, remain poor. In some market economies, the government intervenes in the market to compensate for inequities by providing services such as social security, unemployment insurance, safety standards, minimum wage platforms, and so on.

Socialism in China is designed to reduce the disparity between rich and poor. There are few private automobiles, and there is little production of luxury goods. But food, medicine and housing, the basic necessities, are all kept rather inexpensive by price controls and by political decisions (rather than market decisions).

If a problem with the market system is that it tends to perpetuate inequalities, there are also problems with the socialist system. Decision making tends to become over-centralized, reducing the freedom of choice and creativity of numerous producers. (Such can also happen when a market system is dominated by monopolies or huge conglomerates). It is also extremely difficult for the planners to have sufficient data and sufficient wisdom to plan intelligently for the whole society.

In a market economy each enterprise plans only for itself. Mistakes in a planned, socialist economy tend to have a far wider impact on the whole economy.

Despite these problems, there is little evidence that China will not maintain a basic socialist orientation, but current indications are that increasingly it will try to modify its negative effects by introducing "capitalist" practices, such as decentralizing decision making, letting individual enterprises keep and reinvest their profits instead of turning them over to the government, and letting the market play a bigger role in setting prices and determining what goods will be produced.

The World's Largest
Population

≈§ *Editor's Introduction:* China has the world's largest population, estimated at one billion people in 1981. Almost one of every four people in the world is Chinese. That staggering fact affects almost every decision made in China. Plans for agriculture, industry, education, health, housing and employment are all influenced by population size and population estimates for the future.

In the past several years, China has made a special effort to slow down its population growth rate, and to a great extent it has succeeded. Today China's population is growing at the rate of 1.2 percent a year, one of the lowest growth rates in the developing world and down from 2.0 percent only 10 years ago. (The 1981 U.S. growth rate was 0.7 percent).

However, 1.2 percent of one billion is 12 million, a huge number of people to add to the population each year. The Chinese government has officially committed itself to lowering the growth rate to 1 percent by the end of the century; some official statements have set 1985 as the target year. Family-planning clinics, offering a variety of contraceptives, including abortions, have spread throughout the countryside in recent years, and the government has used every publicity technique at its disposal to encourage couples to marry at a later age, thereby reducing the number of their childbearing years. Already, China's efforts are being studied by other nations as examples of what can be done to solve the world's population problem.

Large families were much desired in traditional China. Because many children died before reaching maturity, many were wanted. Sons were needed to work on the land, to provide old-age security

Huang Yu-chuan, "Birth Control Education Campaigns," in *Population and Family Planning in the People's Republic of China,* The Victor-Bostrom Fund and The Population Crisis Committee, Washington, 1971.

for their parents, to carry on ancestral rites, and to perpetuate the family name. Daughters were not considered so important as sons because they married into other families when they were of age, but even so, they could bring power and prestige to the family and clan through marriage. For economic, social, and religious reasons, then, Chinese parents felt it was their responsibility to have large families.

Conditions have changed radically in China, but some Chinese parents continue to follow the old pattern of having large families. How can this be changed? The following selection describes some of the current efforts of the Chinese government to transform the old patterns of marriage and childbearing.

According to this account, how has China attempted to lower its birth rate? How important has the Communist Party been in this process? ટેસ

The Birth-Control Campaign

"EXTOL ONE, Praise Two, Criticize Three, and Dispose Four."

Slogans, posters, and mass educational theories like this have been a vital part of Chinese birth-control activity. No sooner is a birth-control campaign decided upon than propaganda work begins on a big scale. This was the case in 1956-57 during the first birth-control effort and again in 1962-66 . . .

The younger generation is the main target of Chinese birth-control propaganda. This makes good sense because all those entering their childbearing years after the mid-1960s were born under the present regime and are not as strongly bound by traditional practices. Many of the older generation still like the idea of having many sons and grandsons. They do not want their own sons and daughters to practice birth control.

Also, under the old moral code, Chinese men and women always kept an arm's distance from each other. It is still not easy to discuss sex and contraception openly. The young couples, though more easily influenced, still hesitate to speak publicly about contraceptives or to buy them in a shop. Some are afraid contraceptives will lead to illicit sexual relations and decline in public morality.

When the birth-control campaign was first started, many people felt shy when purchasing contraceptives at the drugstore, especially when the sales personnel were of the opposite sex, so they often left without buying them. For this reason, local drugstores have on duty both men and women to receive customers . . . .

Campaigns for late marriage are an important part of the program and, of course, are aimed at the young. Age of marriage used to be about fifteen or sixteen. In 1950, marriage laws raised the age of marriage to twenty for men and eighteen for women. In 1956 and 1957, there was discussion of raising the age still higher; in 1962, propaganda was stepped up. Students were not allowed to marry until they finished their studies; young people with government jobs might be dismissed from work [if they married]; peasants were discouraged by marriage registrars. Younger couples might not get rations for themselves or their newborn babies.

At the same time, to inspire the people, Chinese Communist publications recounted many stories of exemplary citizens who postponed marriage five or six times. One woman cadre, a local brigade leader, who put off her own marriage six times, was cited as a model to the girls in her brigade. Many pledged to emulate her and not marry until they reached twenty-five. Age twenty-five for women and thirty for men is now the recommended minimum . . . .

Exhibitions are a popular form of education, readily received by the masses and easily moved from place to place. Exhibitions held in cities are fine in quality while those for the villages are comparatively simple. Usually, someone is around to offer point-by-point, picture-by-picture explanations, bearing in mind the cultural level of the masses.

Many of the audience, particularly the rural folk, visit the exhibition with a sense of curiosity or a feeling of shyness. After their visit they acquire some knowledge about birth control. Particularly when thousands upon thousands of men and women, young and old, gather together to visit the exhibition and listen to the explanations, their misgivings of all kinds are more easily dispelled. This produces a tremendous effect in promoting birth control.

The most effective among all forms of propaganda is the individual approach. When the movement was widely unfolded throughout the nation, all the basic-level cadres or activists became the backbone of the propaganda. The health workers, personnel cadres, street representatives, and women representatives in the city organizations and enterprises, on the one hand, and the commune member cadres, Communist Youth League cadres, women representatives, and health workers in the rural areas, on the other, first carried out large-scale propaganda. They then approached individually those parents with many children who were experiencing living difficulties, those about to get married, and those mothers-in-law who would not let their daughters-in-law practice birth control. Because they work in the same unit, live together, and know one another well enough to talk without any reservation, such approaches, when repeatedly made, are difficult to resist.

A family outing in South China. (From China Reconstructs, *August, 1972.)*

The huge number of cadres sent down to the countryside in recent years has become a great force for propaganda on birth control . . . .

The propaganda carried out during the mid-1960s campaign often savored of coercion. For instance, there was the slogan, "Two children is just right, three is too many, and four is a mistake"; no ration ticket for clothing was issued to a third newborn baby; and too-early marriages would not be registered. These measures, conducted and led by certain localities, resulted in workers and employees with many children receiving fewer economic benefits. They also form a strong pressure to make people realize deeply that having too many children is not only a disadvantage to themselves but also an offense to the government. It will be subject to criticism and considered as committing "an error." Therefore, like it or not, practicing birth control has become a social trend for everyone. When this practice becomes a tradition, it is easy for one to rid himself of dissatisfaction and misgiving . . . .

Not only the masses motivated to accept the idea, but also the cadres doing the propaganda work have to practice birth control. The following serves to illustrate this point:

A man cadre working in one of the newspapers already was a father of three children. He and his wife both wanted sterilization. Said his wife, "Surgically, the tying of the vas deferens is much easier for men to undergo, but, entertaining the fear that they will be physically affected if the operation is not successful, they always let their wives undergo an operation." When her colleagues learned of this, they criticized her husband, saying, "A husband that does not go for an operation but asks his wife to have it is selfish and is affected by the thinking that men are more important than women." Her husband said, "You hit the nail on the head by criticizing me this way." He felt ashamed of himself, for his wife, being a Party member and also chief of a production brigade, labors well, keeps the house well, and performs a duty that is heavier than his own. So he decided right away to have the operation.

The above instance shows that, although the decision on birth control has to be made by the couple themselves, it is apparent that certain pressure is brought to bear. This kind of propaganda method, which combines pressure with commendation, is precisely what the Chinese Communists have all along stressed . . . .

✒ *Editor's Postscript:* Since this article was written, stricter measures have been taken to control population growth. In many areas, especially in cities, a third child will be alloted no ration card for food or clothing and the family will have to pay for its education. The family will also be given very low priority for new housing, even though its housing needs are greater. ✑

The Environment: Two Views

✍§ *Editor's Introduction:* As China's population and its economy grow, environmental questions become increasingly important. Until recently the Chinese have been optimistic about this issue. Speaking at the United Nations in 1973, a Chinese delegate said:

> [We] would . . . like to deal briefly with the relationship between population growth and protection of the human environment. We hold that of all things in the world, people are the most precious. The masses have boundless creative power. To develop social production and create social wealth depends on people, and to improve the human environment also depends on people. The history of mankind has proved that the pace of development of production, science, and technology always surpasses the rate of population growth. The possibility of man's exploitation and utilization of natural resources is inexhaustible.
>
> Moreover, with the progress in science and technology, man's use of natural resources will increasingly grow in depth and scope. Mankind will create ever-greater quantities of wealth to meet the needs of its own subsistence and development. Mankind's ability to transform the environment will also grow continuously along with social progress and the advance of science and technology.°

The delegates' optimism is reflected in an article written in the Peking Review in 1973, but it is seriously challenged by a Canadian professor writing in 1980. Can the two views be reconciled? &»

° "China Explains Her Views on the Population Question," *Peking Review*, April 27, 1973, p. 17; abridged.

"Industrial Development and Pollution Control," *China Reconstructs*, February, 1973, pp. 2-5; abridged.

A Chinese View

CHINA IS NOW working in a planned way to prevent and eliminate industrial pollution of the environment by what we call the "three wastes"—waste gases, liquids, and residues. A good beginning has been made on this in the past few years.

REDISTRIBUTION OF INDUSTRY

We are pursuing a policy of building more industrial towns elsewhere in order to avoid overconcentration of industry and population in the older big cities. This means less industrial waste and garbage to be disposed of in any one place. It also facilitates the policy of combining industry and agriculture, city and country.

NEW-TYPE OIL TOWNS

The Taching oilfield provides an example. In its early days an argument arose about what kind of residential community it should have . . . .

A proposal to build a big city was discarded. Instead, more than a hundred smaller communities were set up scattered over a vast area between the extraction districts. The workers can be closer to their jobs and their families can be organized for work on the land nearby. The latter have now reclaimed about 10,000 hectares, on which are produced thousands of tons of grain and vegetables annually. Such communities of simple, conveniently located dwellings not only provide a more healthful environment for the workers to live in but also make for the combination of industry and agriculture, city and country.

TRANSFORMING OLD CITIES

Old industrial cities are gradually being transformed. Take Shanghai, for instance, where, before the liberation, imperialist capital built factories to plunder China's resources and exploit her cheap labor-power. Factories located in and among areas where the working people lived spewed forth their poisonous smoke, emptied out their poisonous residues, and dumped their refuse without restriction, creating a very unhealthful atmosphere. After liberation, the people's government began transforming China's largest city into a new socialist one.

The first stage included covering the open sewage channels and building boulevards above them. Three hundred miserable slum areas were torn down and new "workers' village" housing projects constructed on the sites, providing new homes for over a million people.

A second measure was to adjust the distribution of industry. About 1,000 factories located near residential areas were considered particularly harmful. These were rather small factories using crude equipment and backward technological processes. During the First Five-Year Plan (1953-57) the government began moving most of these outside the city and renovating them to reduce pollution, improve working conditions, and facilitate production.

When new industrial plants are set up, they are constructed outside the city. New industrial districts for chemicals, electrical machinery, instruments and meters, metallurgy, and oil refining have been set up at distances up to twenty kilometers, from the city. A "buffer zone" between them and the city helps curtail pollution in the inner city.

UTILIZING WASTE

Full utilization of wastes—converting hazards into benefits—is another important measure. Some progress has been made in this respect. Tail gas from oil refineries used to be poured into the air. Now from this gas many petrochemical units recover valuable chemicals used in making things like synthetic fibers and rubber, plastics and chemical fertilizers. Coal rocks and slag, which, when dumped, formerly covered huge areas of farmland, are now being used in the production of chemical raw materials, fertilizers, cement, bricks, and refractory materials. From the toxic tail gas from nonferrous-metals refining, large amounts of sulphuric acid are being recovered. Several hundred products are now being made out of wastes from chemical, insecticide, pharmaceutical, and

Going to work, Peking. (From New China News Agency, Peking.)

light industrial production.

    The recovery and utilization of wastes is an integral part of national planning for basic construction. Projects for this purpose are required to go into operation at the same time that new factories and mines go into production. Industrial departments are working together with research units to improve production processes so as to reduce or eliminate pollution. Research is also being done on ways to counteract the harm caused by remaining health hazards and to find ways of treating diseases caused by them.

ALL FOR THE PEOPLE

In our country, what benefits the people and the country is given first consideration in everything that is done. Therefore some areas and enterprises allocate a certain portion of their funds for treatment of sewage and other wastes. This may yield them little or no profit, but from the point of view of the whole, of preventing pollution of the air, rivers and water sources, protecting aquatic life and supporting agriculture, this means great profit indeed. Therefore these departments do so readily . . . .

The Chinese people are keenly aware that only by building an independent national industry can the people's livelihood be continuously improved and the country made strong and prosperous. Growth of industry is bound to present greater environmental problems. Social progress and the advance of science and technology can help solve them. We believe, however, that the key to solving them is action by the masses—that is, bringing their initiative and wisdom into full play on the principle of "everything to benefit the people."

China has made some progress in eliminating pollution, but we still do not have much experience. And even when old problems of waste are solved, the use of new materials, technological processes, and techniques and the development of new products will create more problems. Ending environmental pollution is indeed a long-term project.

An Outside View

A very disquieting picture of China's environment has emerged as a result of the recent openness of the Peking leadership. China faces pollution and environmental degradation at least as serious as in any large modernizing nation and the current plans for fast, large scale industrialization in the coming decades cannot but worsen the situation.

The recent Chinese admissions are in sharp contrast to

Vaclav Smil, "The Four Modernizations: Smog, Oil Slicks, Noise, Waste," *The Asian Wall Street Journal*, Nov. 20, 1980.

writings and broadcasts of just a few years ago when, in
Maoist phrases, only the "monopoly capitalist groups which
seek superprofits" were the ones discharging "at will and in
disregard of the fate of the people harmful substances that
pollute and poison the environment." Now the State
Economic Commission and the Office for Environmental
Protection of the State Council are expressing concern about
serious environmental deterioration and are trying to check
the tide of problems that have been accumulating for
decades.

SMOG

Air pollution is a ubiquitous and particularly troublesome
problem in virtually all of China's large cities and industrial
areas. The widespread burning of low-quality solid fuels is its
principal source. China is extracting over 600 million tons of
raw coal and uses nearly one-third of this output as household
fuel, either as lump coal or coal-dust briquettes.

Combustion of these inferior fuels in small stoves is
inefficient, and the pollutants are released without much
dispersion very low above the ground, making for a most
intractable air quality problem, especially in China's northern
cities. High winter concentrations of soot and sulfur dioxide
are responsible for large numbers of people suffering from
chronic respiratory diseases. Industrial coal combustion is a
no less serious contributor to China's air pollution. In Peking,
where over 8 million tons of coal are consumed annually, 72%
of the fuel burned in industrial enterprises is wasted and such
low efficiency is typical across the country.

The most difficult problem in the future will be the
gaseous pollution (sulfur dioxide and nitrogen oxides) that
will spread over large areas as a result of the planned
expansion of coal-fired electricity generation in huge modern
power plants. Using bituminous coal and low quality high-
sulfur lignite as fuel for power plants is a national strategy, and
the Chinese are already committed to the construction of a
series of giant coal-fired stations in several provinces.

Currently there are no reliable and inexpensive ways to

control sulfur dioxide from such large plants. The resulting acid rain will have especially damaging effects on crop yields, in particular on vegetables grown in suburban areas, and it will have major destabilizing effects on aquaculture.

NOISE

Noise pollution in large Chinese cities is astounding: taxis in Peking and Shanghai are hooting their horns at a fairly constant rate, one beep per car every 1.2 seconds. The situation is not helped by the habit of turning off the engine at red traffic lights to save fuel. Ma Dayou, deputy director of the Chinese Academy of Sciences Institute of Acoustics, says noise in Peking is worse than in Tokyo, a city with 15 times the number of vehicles and many more factories and transport terminals than China's capital. He adds that measurements in other large cities showed the average decibel level to be higher in Peking than in New York, London, Rome or Tokyo.

WATER POLLUTION

With the rapid expansion of the energy, chemical, and metallurgical industries and with the growth of cities, there is widespread water pollution. All major rivers have been seriously contaminated in the stretches in and downstream of cities that discharge large quantities of untreated industrial and urban waste. Even more alarmingly, contamination of Bo Hai, China's largest bay, is becoming serious and it will most likely deteriorate further once the large-scale expansion of petroleum production from the undersea extensions of Dagang and Shengli oilfields gets under way with the much more frequent oil tanker traffic.

China's marine life has been already damaged by indiscriminate fishing methods and by land reclamation along the coast. Catches of several fish species have fallen substantially and some popular kinds, such as yellow croaker, are becoming extinct.

Reclaiming of land along coasts traditionally used for seafood breeding or as natural feeding and spawning grounds has destroyed precious resources. A total of over 60,000 hectares* of such land was reclaimed between 1959 and 1978 and large losses of high quality sea protein cannot ever be made up by the meagre crop yields from the inappropriately reclaimed land.

Incomparably greater damage was done to freshwater fishing. Incomplete statistics indicate that since 1949, 8% of China's total inland water surface has been lost to indiscriminate land reclamation.

The fish catch from inland waters has fallen to only half that of 1954, making fresh fish a rare delicacy in a nation where aquatic protein used to be a close second to pork, and first in many places. Moreover production of valuable reeds, lotus roots, water chestnuts, and weeds has been lost, floodwater retention reduced, and local climate disturbed.

Disappearance of good farmland is a universal problem, but for China—a nation with less than 0.1 hectare of cultivated land per capita—it is an extremely perilous trend. In 1957 China's cultivated area was 111.8 million hectares, but during 1979 many Chinese sources kept referring to only 100 million hectares, implying that 12% of the country's farmland had been lost in just over two decades. The irrationality of Chinese land use is all too obvious: tens of millions of people are straining themselves every winter and spring to reclaim much of the inferior land in distant mountain regions, on hill slopes, in waterlogged, alkaline or saline areas while millions of hectares of prime farmland are disappearing.

Conversion of grasslands to cropland, practiced for two decades on a large scale, has had predictable consequences. Once the natural vegetation is destroyed the ecosystem balance is lost, yields of newly introduced crops swiftly fall, and the land is condemned to inexorable erosion and desertification.

Although an eighth of China is covered with forest, it is extremely unevenly distributed. More than half is either a secondary regrowth or young plantings. The Chinese have undertaken massive afforestation campaigns officially claim-

---

* One hectare equals 2.5 acres.

ing up to 28 million hectares of newly afforested land since 1949.

Naive foreigners have taken these claims at face value, not realizing that all too often they represent targets passed down from above whose fulfillment was, in due time, reported by lower-level bureaucrats no matter how the work was done, if at all. A revealing folk saying explains why some areas plant trees every year—and still have no forests: "Trees everywhere in spring, just half left by summer; no care taken in the fall, all trees gone by winter." The survival rate of new plantings has been appallingly low, often much below 10%, for several reasons: Careless planting, inadequate follow-up care and lack of a scientific approach to afforestation.

But many trees that survive are recklessly destroyed to obtain scarce fuel: branches are cut off, roots dug up and bark and leaves torn off. Illegal felling of mature trees in state forests, always strictly forbidden by both state and provincial regulations, has become so widespread lately that the State Council has had to issue a new law that not only imposes fines and planting of three new trees for every one destroyed but also demands a guarantee of the new saplings' survival.

Forests in many areas are in a poor state and are still being damaged; commercial logging increases while large areas of cutover forest have not yet been reforested; consequently, in the past few years forest resources have gradually diminished and a 1979 national symposium on forestry economics was told that "according to the estimate based on the actual rate of reduction, by the end of this century there will be no trees to harvest."

The costs involved in reversing environmental degradation will not be low. The Chinese have achieved no mean results in eliminating various wastes through simple and frugal recycling, but pollution from large, modern industries can be handled only by introducing the appropriate advanced technologies. Many of these are complex, expensive and energy-intensive and will increase China's modernization costs appreciably.

But the Chinese have hardly any other choice. Uncontrolled pollution would soon lead to drastic decreases of crop and livestock production, extinction of aquatic life and irreparable damage to forests. The Chinese also have to stop and reverse the conversion of grasslands, lakes, and coastal areas to crop fields, manage their forests much more carefully and proceed cautiously with chemization of their food chains.

How well it can balance the conflicting requirements of speedy industrialization and higher agricultural production with the necessity of a reasonably clean environment is one of the main dilemmas China faces along the road to development.

Barefoot Doctors

Editor's Introduction: Population and environmental issues are closely related to health considerations. In contrast to the dispute over environmental issues discussed in the last chapter, there is general agreement that medical care has made great progress.

In the years following the establishment of the People's Republic in 1949, a number of measures were taken that greatly improved the general health of the populace. Techniques of mass organization and education, which had been used effectively to bring the Communists to power, were employed in nationwide campaigns to improve sanitation and hygiene, eliminate disease-bearing pests, and immunize the populace against contagious diseases.

As a result of these efforts, epidemics of smallpox, cholera, and plague that had flourished during the long years of war were quickly brought under control; cases of tuberculosis and schistosomiasis (a seriously debilitating disease caused by snails) fell sharply; drug addiction and venereal disease were virtually eliminated, at a time when they were spreading rapidly in other parts of the world.

The government subsidized the cost of medical care, reducing or eliminating direct costs to the patient. For employees of state-run enterprises, such as factories, mines, railroads, and government offices, and for students, medical care is free except for a small registration fee of about 3¢ (U.S. equivalent in 1973). Peasants are covered by cooperative medical plans to which they contribute 25¢ to 50¢ per year. Dependents and other nonworking people who are

" 'Barefoot Doctors'—Giving Medical Treatment While Taking Part in Farm Work," *Peking Review*, May 25, 1973, pp. 15-21; abridged.

not covered by these plans pay a very small fee for health care. A chest x-ray costs about 8¢, a hospital bed costs 25¢ or less per day. The cost for delivering a child is about $1.25, an appendectomy costs $2.00, and the most difficult operations, such as heart or brain surgery, cost less than $8.00.

The cost of medicines is also low and has been reduced continually since 1949. Most prescriptions today cost 1 ¢ or less.

By the mid-1960s, the health of the Chinese people had greatly improved, but a major unsolved problem, which became a central issue of dispute during the Cultural Revolution, was the uneven distribution of medical care. As in most countries, doctors and medical supplies were in greater abundance in the cities than in the countryside. In many rural areas, medical care was inadequate or nonexistent. As a result of the Cultural Revolution, much more attention has been given to rural areas, where most of the people live. Many doctors have been transferred to rural areas to live and work, but because there are too few fully trained M.D.'s to service the whole population, the emphasis has been on training tens of thousands of paramedical personnel, called "barefoot doctors."

The selections that follow describe the function of those barefoot doctors. How are they trained? How would a large corps of paramedical personnel affect the delivery of medical care in the United States? ᘐ

THE NAME "barefoot doctor" first appeared in the Chiang-chen People's Commune on Shanghai's outskirts.

In 1965, when Chairman Mao issued the call "In medical and health work, put the stress on the rural areas," a number of mobile medical teams formed by urban medical workers came to Chiang-chen. Though it was near the metropolis, this commune had only one health clinic with about a dozen medical personnel serving a population of 28,000. When the medical teams arrived, the local peasants were glad to see them. While curing and preventing commune members' diseases, the doctors from Shanghai helped the clinic give a group of young peasants some medical training.

Later, when the teams left, these peasants took their place and since then have gradually become full-fledged doctors. Taking medical kits with them, they worked barefooted alongside the peasants in the paddyfields, and they treated peasants in the fields, on the threshing grounds, or in their homes. They were at once commune members and doctors, doing farm work and treating patients. Like other commune members, they receive their pay on the basis of workpoints, and their income was more or less the same as that of able-bodied peasants doing the same amount of work. The peasants warmly welcomed them and affectionately called them "barefoot doctors.". . . .

Generally speaking, "barefoot doctors" are given three to six months of short-term training before starting to work. Training classes with few but well-selected courses are run by the commune's clinic, county hospital, and mobile medical teams from the cities or medical schools. . . . The aim is to give the trainees the ability to do practical work as quickly as possible and to lay the foundation for advanced study. . . .

In 1965, Wang Kuei-chen, who was twenty-one that year, was chosen to attend a training course for "barefoot doctors" run by the commune's clinic. . . .

During her four months of training, Wang Kuei-chen and twenty-seven other young men and women were taught to cure scores of common diseases and to prescribe some 100 medicines. . . . They learned the fundamentals of acupuncture treatment at thirty major points on the human body. This ABC of medical science was of great use to these young people, who have deep feelings for the peasants.

Back from the training course, Wang Kuei-chen continued doing farm work, such as transplanting rice-shoots, weeding, and harvesting together with the villagers. Wherever she worked, in the fields, at construction sites of water-conservancy projects, or other places, she always had her medical kit at hand. She and two other "barefoot doctors" took charge of handling all the diseases and injuries they could among the more than 1,500 brigade members. After giving prescriptions, she made it a rule to call on the patients and ask them about the effects of the medicine so as to sum up experience and improve her work. As to cases she could not handle, she always went with the patients to the city hospital. . . .

All this was not just for the purpose of learning, but, more important, her aim was to look after the patients still better. In summer, villagers sometimes were bitten by snakes. When she was told that a worker in a factory several kilometers away could treat snakebites with herbal medicine, she immediately went to see him. Combining what she learned from the worker with Western medicine, she has treated more than a dozen snakebite cases in the last two years.

Affectionately called their "close friend" by the villagers, Wang Kuei-chen was elected deputy secretary of the com-

An old doctor trains a barefoot doctor to recognize medicinal herbs. (*From* China Reconstructs, *November, 1972.*)

mune Party committee and a member of the county Party committee. Despite the change in her position, she is still a "barefoot doctor."

She has also made rapid progress in medical technique. She and other "barefoot doctors" took turns working in the commune's health clinic or getting further training in advanced courses. Last year, she spent two months studying anatomy, physiology, and biochemistry in a medical college and later went to the county hospital's internal medicine department for advanced study in combination with clinical treatment.

"Barefoot doctor" Chang Hsiang-hua in the countryside . . . in northwest China had only learned some elementary knowledge and technique of Western medicine in a training class. In the course of practice, he found that there were many effective prescriptions of traditional Chinese medicine used by the local people who lived in a hilly village where many medicinal herbs grew. If these traditional methods were put to good use, he thought, it would produce very good results in curing certain diseases and save the patients much expense. So he and his colleagues set about learning from veteran practitioners of traditional Chinese medicine and experienced herbpickers in the locality. As a result, they were able to recognize 240 herbs and learned to give herbal prescriptions and cure diseases by acupuncture. They themselves picked the needed herbs and later planted them. Last year, they went a step further. . . . They processed herbs into easy-to-use pills, powders, and liquid medicines to stop bleeding and coughing, induce lactation, and cure burns.

In 1970, Chang Hsiang-hua had the opportunity to learn from a traditional Chinese doctor of a medical team that had come from Peking for six months. He worked together with this old doctor every day, diagnosing and curing patients. He also spent one to two hours listening to his talks on the theories of traditional Chinese medicine. Studying this way helped Chang quickly increase his ability.

For a period of time, he and other "barefoot doctors" in

the brigade cooperated closely with medical teams from Pe-king, making an over-all investigation of an endemic disease. They learned to give every brigade member a cardiographic check-up and carried out auscultatory and oral investigations from house to house. They gave decoctions of herbal medicine twice a day to twenty-eight patients who had varying symptoms. Carefully observing the effects, they continued studying ways to improve the prescription's ingredients. After 150 days, all the patients were better. In this way, the young "barefoot doctors" learned how to diagnose, cure, treat and prevent this disease.

Study through practice, as shown by the above-mentioned examples, is the basic way "barefoot doctors" are trained. This quick and effective method makes up for the drawbacks owing to medical schools' being unable to train large numbers of doctors in a short time. In a developing country like China, the first step to change backwardness in medical work in the rural areas is, so to speak, "sending charcoal in snowy weather," not "adding flowers to the embroidery." "Barefoot doctors" are a newborn force that has bright prospects.

Every rural people's commune today has its "barefoot doctors" who are either children of the once-impoverished peasants and herdsmen or city-bred middle-school students who have settled in the countryside. These peasant-doctors are playing an important role in the rural areas where doctors and medicine are in great demand.

"Never the Twain Shall Meet"

⌐ૐ *Editor's Introduction:* For many years after the establishment of the People's Republic, China's relations with the rest of the world were severely restricted. Practically its only friends were the Soviet Union and other Communist countries. The United States vowed both to contain and isolate China, viewing it as a pawn in the Soviet Union's alleged desire to dominate and transform the world. China's confrontation with United Nations forces in the Korean War, in the early 1950s, served to confirm suspicions of Chinese aggressiveness.

From the Chinese perspective, the Korean War, and the French military effort to regain control in Indo-China (Vietnam, Laos and Cambodia) on China's southern border confirmed its suspicion that Western imperialists were still trying to dominate Asia, as they had before World War II.

In the late 1950s and early 1960s when its relations with the Soviet Union deteriorated, China became even more isolated. Unwilling to accept satellite status under Soviet domination, like the Eastern European countries, China turned to a policy of self-reliance. Its commercial and political relations with other countries practically halted, especially during the Cultural Revolution when China recalled all but one of its ambassadors. Not until the early 1970s did China begin to reestablish foreign contacts.

China's isolation, then, was imposed both from the outside and from inside. To understand the situation in depth, one must look at history. Traditionally, the Chinese wanted very little to do with foreigners. They considered them barbarians from whom they had little to gain materially or culturally. Foreign diplomats were accepted by the Chinese emperor only if they acknowledged their inferiority and begged to be educated.

In the 19th century, Europeans and Americans wanted both

diplomatic equality and trade, and were willing to fight to get them. Having defeated the Chinese in the Opium War in 1840, Westerners began to despise the Chinese for their weakness.

In the readings which follow, the arrogance of the traditional Chinese attitude toward foreigners, illustrated in the letter from the Ch'ien Lung Emperor to King George of England in 1793, is matched by the arrogance of Westerners once they had become dominant in China, illustrated in excerpts from speeches by U.S. Senator Albert Beveridge, President Theodore Roosevelt, and Kaiser Wilhelm II of Germany whose troops were about to lead a punitive expedition against the Chinese in 1900. These selections were all written in the late 19th and early 20th Century. ঽ

Edict from the Ch'ien-Lung Emperor
To King George III of England

[September 1793, on the Occasion of Lord Macartney's Mission to China]

You, O King, live beyond the confines of many seas, nevertheless, impelled by your humble desire to partake of the benefits of our civilization, you have dispatched a mission respectfully bearing your memorial. Your Envoy has crossed the seas and paid his respects at my Court on the anniversary of my birthday. To show your devotion, you have also sent offerings of your country's produce.

I have perused your memorial: the earnest terms in which it is couched reveal a respectful humility on your part, which is highly praiseworthy. In consideration of the fact that your Ambassador and his deputy have come a long way with your memorial and tribute, I have shown them high favour and have allowed them to be introduced into my presence. To manifest my indulgence, I have entertained them at a banquet and made them numerous gifts. I have also caused presents to be forwarded to the Naval Commander and six hundred of his officers and men, although they did not come to Peking, so that they too may share in my all-embracing kindness.

As to your entreaty to send one of your nationals to be accredited to my Celestial Court and to be in control of your

Dun J. Ki, *Modern China, From Mandarin to Commisar,* Charles Scribner and Sons, New York, 1978, pp. 41-45.

country's trade with China, this request is contrary to all usage of my dynasty and cannot possibly be entertained. It is true that Europeans, in the service of the dynasty, have been permitted to live at Peking, but they are compelled to adopt Chinese dress, they are strictly confined to their own precincts and are never permitted to return home. You are presumably familiar with our dynastic regulations. Your proposed Envoy to my Court could not be placed in a position similar to that of European officials in Peking who are forbidden to leave China, nor could he, on the other hand, be allowed liberty of movement and the privilege of corresponding with his own country; so that you would gain nothing by his residence in our midst.

Moreover, Our Celestial dynasty possesses vast territories, and tribute missions from the dependencies are provided for by the Department for Tributary States, which ministers to their wants and exercises strict control over their movements. It would be quite impossible to leave them to their own devices. Supposing that your Envoy should come to our Court, his language and national dress differ from that of our people, and there would be no place in which he might reside. It may be suggested that he might imitate the Europeans permanently resident in Peking and adopt the dress and customs of China, but, it has never been our dynasty's wish to force people to do things unseemly and inconvenient. Besides, supposing I sent an Ambassador to reside in your country, how could you possibly make for him the requisite arrangements? Europe consists of many other nations besides your own: if each and all demanded to be represented at our Court, how could we possibly consent? The thing is utterly impracticable. How can our dynasty alter its whole procedure and regulations, established for more than a century, in order to meet your individual views? If it be said that your object is to exercise control over your country's trade, your nationals have had full liberty to trade at Canton for many a year, and have received the greatest consideration at our hands. Missions have been sent by Portugal and Italy, preferring similar requests. The Throne appreciated their

A women's militia artillery unit. (*From* Jen-min hua-pao, *Nos. 7–8, 1971, p. 15.*)

sincerity and loaded them with favours, besides authorising measures to facilitate their trade with China. You are no doubt aware that, when my Canton merchant, Wu Chao-p'ing, was in debt to the foreign ships, I made the Viceroy advance the monies due, out of the provincial treasury, and ordered him to punish the culprit severely. Why then should foreign nations advance this utterly unreasonable request to be represented at my Court? Peking is nearly 10,000 *li* from Canton, and at such a distance what possible control could any British representative exercise?

If you assert that your reverence for Our Celestial dynasty fills you with a desire to acquire our civilisation, our ceremonies and code of laws differ so completely from your own that, even if your Envoy were able to acquire the rudiments of our civilisation, you could not possibly transplant our manners and customs to your alien soil. Therefore, however adept the Envoy might become, nothing would be gained thereby.

Swaying the wide world, I have but one aim in view, namely, to maintain a perfect governance and to fulfil the duties of the State; strange and costly objects do not interest me. If I have commanded that the tribute offerings sent by you, O King, are to be accepted, this was solely in consideration for the spirit which prompted you to dispatch them from afar. Our dynasty's majestic virtue has penetrated unto every country under Heaven, and Kings of all nations have offered their costly tribute by land and sea. As your Ambassador can see for himself, we possess all things. I set no value on objects strange or ingenious, and have no use for your country's manufactures. This then is my answer to your request to appoint a representative at my Court, a request contrary to our dynastic usage, which would only result in inconvenience to yourself. I have expounded my wishes in detail and have commanded your tribute Envoys to leave in peace on their homeward journey. It behoves you, O King, to respect my sentiments and to display even greater devotion and loyalty in the future, so that, by perpetual submission to our Throne, you may secure peace and prosperity for your country hereafter. Besides making gifts (of which I enclose a list) to each member of your Mission, I confer upon you, O King, valuable presents in excess of the number usually bestowed on such occasions, including silks and curios—a list of which is likewise enclosed. Do you reverently receive them and take note of my tender goodwill towards you! A special mandate.

Albert Beveridge (1898)

" . . . He (Grant) never forgot that we are a conquering race and that we must obey our blood and occupy new markets, and if necessary, new lands. He beheld as a part of the Almighty's infinite plan, the disappearance of debased civilizations and decaying races before the higher civilization of the nobler and more virile types of man.

"Fate puts the American people upon their decision between a Chinese policy of isolation, poverty, and decay, or an American policy of progress, prosperity, and power.

"And in freeing Peoples, perishing and oppressed, our country's blessing will also come; for profits follow righteousness."

Theodore Roosevelt (1900)

" . . . We cannot, if we would, play the part of China, and be content to rot by inches in ignoble ease within our borders, taking no interest in what goes beyond them; sunk in a scrambling commercialism; heedless of the *higher* life, the life of aspiration, of toil and risk; busying ourselves only with the wants of our bodies for the day; until suddenly we should find, beyond a shadow of question, what China has already found, that in this world the nation that has trained itself to a career of unwarlike and isolated ease is bound in the end to go down before other nations which have not lost the manly and adventurous qualities."

Kaiser Wilhelm II (1900)

" . . . By nature the Chinaman is a cowardly cur, but he is tricky and double-faced. Small detached troops must be particularly cautious. The Chinaman likes to fall upon an enemy from an ambush, or during night time, or with vast superiority in numbers. Recently the enemy has fought bravely, a fact which has not yet been sufficiently explained. Perhaps these were his best troops, drilled by German and other officers.

"The Chinese have disregarded the law of nations. They

have shown scorn for the sacredness of an envoy, for the duties of hospitality, in a manner unparalleled in the history. And this the more reprehensible because these crimes have been committed by a nation which boasts of its ancient culture . . . . You are to fight against a cunning, courageous, well-armed, and cruel foe. When you are upon him, know this: spare nobody, make no prisoners. See your weapons in a manner to make every Chinaman for a thousand years to come forego the wish to as much as look askance at a German . . . ."

China and the United States

An American View of China in 1966

☙*Editor's Introduction:* In 1972, President Nixon visited China, and for the first time since 1949 the hostility that had marked relations between the United States and the People's Republic of China began to abate. The American people began to take a closer look at China and to see some admirable things. The Chinese press became less abusive in its remarks about the United States and even declared that there were things that the Chinese could learn from America.

The differences between the two countries are by no means resolved. They will continue to influence international relations for the indefinite future. But for the first time in more than two decades, the two nations are willing to discuss their differences openly, face to face.

The reasons for hostility between the United States and the People's Republic are very complex, but we can get some insight into them by reading statements that both sides have made. In the selection that follows, written in 1966, the American Assistant Secretary of State for Far Eastern Affairs gives his view of Chinese intentions in foreign affairs. Why does he think China is to be feared?☙

THERE IS TODAY in Communist China a government whose leadership is dedicated to the promotion of Communism by violent revolution.

William P. Bundy, "The United States and Communist China," Washington, D.C.: U.S. Government Printing Office, 1966; abridged.

The present leaders in Peking also seek to restore China to its past position of grandeur and influence. Many of Peking's leaders today, now grown old, are proud and arrogant, convinced that they have been responsible for a resurgence of Chinese power. The China of old exercised a degree of control over Asia that waxed and waned according to the power of the ruling emperor. Under strong rulers this meant a type of overlordship, sometimes benign but frequently otherwise, over the countries around its borders. And the restoration of that image and controlling influence is certainly a part of Communist China's foreign policy today.

In the 1930's, Mao Tse-tung called attention to areas controlled by China under the Manchu Empire but since removed from Chinese control: Korea, Taiwan, the Ryukyus, the Pescadores, Burma, Bhutan, Nepal, Annam, and Outer Mongolia. In more recent years, Chinese Communist leaders have added to that list parts of Soviet Central Asia and eastern Siberia. I think we can take this as valid evidence of Peking's Asian ambitions. . . .

In addition to these historically rooted aspirations, the present leadership is inspired by a Communist ideology still in a highly militant and aggressive phase. . . .

This Communist element includes the advocacy of change through revolution and violence throughout the world and particularly in China's neighboring areas—not revolution seeking the fruition of the national goals of the people of these areas, but revolution supplied or stimulated from outside and based on a preconceived pattern of historical development.

Their vision of this Communist mission extends to countries far from China—including, as we all clearly have seen, Africa and even Latin America. Peking's plans for carrying out its objectives have been delineated in a series of pronouncements issued by its leaders, one of the latest and most widely publicized having been that issued last September by Marshal Lin Piao, top military leader in Communist China, in which Lin Piao offered Chinese Communist experience in the war against Japan as a lesson to be emulated by the less developed countries in Asia, Africa, and Latin America in their pursuit of "revolution.". . .

[The] spread of Chinese domination would inevitably create its own dynamic and in the end threaten even the most securely based and largest nations within the area of that threat, such as India and Japan. One does not need to subscribe to any pat "domino" formula to know from the history of the last generation, and indeed from all history, that the spread of domination feeds on itself, kindling its own fires within the dominant country and progressively weakening the will and capability of others to resist. . . .

A Chinese View of the United States in 1965

Editor's Introduction: The statement by William Bundy refers to the threat the Chinese pose to world peace and especially to Asia. The Chinese were quick to point out that, at the time that statement was made, not one single Chinese military unit was stationed outside China, but that the United States, by contrast, had surrounded China with military bases in Japan, Okinawa, Korea, the Philippines, and Thailand, and had several thousand fighting troops just over the Chinese border in Vietnam. For Americans, a comparable situation would exist if the Chinese had had major bases in Canada, the Dominican Republic, Cuba, and Nantucket Island, and were fighting a major war against America's allies in Mexico. The Chinese said a look at a map showing where foreign troops are stationed around the world would make it clear who is the aggressor and the threat to world peace.

William Bundy's statement refers to an article by Lin Piao. Part of that article is reproduced below. It puts the aggressor's shoe on the other foot.

In what respects does Lin Piao differ with Secretary Bundy?

SINCE WORLD WAR II, U.S. imperialism has stepped into the shoes of German, Japanese, and Italian fascism and has been trying to build a great American empire by dominating and enslaving the whole world. It is actively fostering Japanese

Lin Piao, *Long Live the Victory of People's War!* (Peking: Foreign Languages Press, 1966), pp. 53–58; abridged.

and West German militarism as its chief accomplices in un-
leashing a world war. Like a vicious wolf, it is bullying and
enslaving various peoples, plundering their wealth, encroach-
ing upon their countries' sovereignty and interfering in their
internal affairs. It is the most rabid aggressor in human history
and the most ferocious common enemy of the people of the
world. Every people or country in the world that wants revolution, independence, and peace cannot but direct the spearhead
of its struggle against U.S. imperialism.

Just as the Japanese imperialists' policy of subjugating
China made it possible for the Chinese people to form the
broadest possible united front against them, so the U.S. imperialists' policy of seeking world domination makes it possible for the people throughout the world to unite all the forces
that can be united and form the broadest possible united front
for a converging attack on U.S. imperialism. . . .

Since World War II, people's war has increasingly demon-
strated its power in Asia, Africa, and Latin America. The peoples of China, Korea, Vietnam, Laos, Cuba, Indonesia, Algeria,
and other countries have waged people's wars against the
imperialists and their lackeys and won great victories. The
classes leading these people's wars may vary, and so may the
breadth and depth of mass mobilization and the extent of
victory, but the victories in these people's wars have very
much weakened and pinned down the forces of imperialism,
upset the U.S. imperialist plan to launch a world war, and
become mighty factors defending world peace.

Today, the conditions are more favorable than ever before for waging of people's wars by the revolutionary peoples
of Asia, Africa, and Latin America against U.S. imperialism
and its lackeys. . . .

When committing aggression in a foreign country, U.S.
imperialism can only employ part of its forces, which are sent
to fight an unjust war far from their native land and therefore
have a low morale, and so U.S. imperialism is beset with great
difficulties. The people subjected to its aggression are having a
trial of strength with U.S. imperialism neither in Washington

nor New York, neither in Honolulu nor Florida, but are fighting for independence and freedom on their own soil. Once they are mobilized on a broad scale, they will have inexhaustible strength. Thus superiority will belong not to the United States but to the people subjected to its aggression. The latter, though apparently weak and small, are really more powerful than U.S. imperialism.

"Ping pong diplomacy"—the first break in Chinese-American hostility was the invitation to the U.S. table tennis team to visit China in 1971.

The struggles waged by the different peoples against U.S. imperialism reinforce each other and merge into a torrential world-wide tide of opposition to U.S. imperialism. The more successful the development of people's war in a given region, the larger the number of U.S. imperialist forces that can be pinned down and depleted there. When the U.S. aggressors are hard-pressed in one place, they have no alternative but to loosen their grip on others. Therefore, the conditions become more favorable for the people elsewhere to wage struggles against U.S. imperialism and its lackeys. . . .

However highly developed modern weapons and technical equipment may be and however complicated the methods of modern warfare, in the final analysis the outcome of a war will be decided by the sustained fighting of the ground forces, by the fighting at close quarters on battlefields, by the political consciousness of the men, by their courage and spirit of sacrifice. Here the weak points of U.S. imperialism will be completely laid bare, while the superiority of the revolutionary people will be brought into full play. The reactionary troops of U.S. imperialism cannot possibly be endowed with the courage and the spirit of sacrifice possessed by the revolutionary people. The spiritual atom bomb that the revolutionary people possess is a far more powerful and useful weapon than the physical atom bomb.

Vietnam is the most convincing current example of a victim of aggression defeating U.S. imperialism by a people's war. The United States had made South Vietnam a testing ground for the suppression of people's war. It has carried on this experiment for many years, and everybody can now see that the U.S. aggressors are unable to find a way of coping with people's war. On the other hand, the Vietnamese people have brought the power of people's war into full play in their struggle against the U.S. aggressors. The U.S. aggressors are in danger of being swamped in the people's war in Vietnam. They are deeply worried that their defeat in Vietnam will lead to a chain reaction. They are expanding the war in an attempt to save themselves from defeat. But the more they expand the war, the greater will be the chain reaction. The more they escalate the war, the heavier will be their fall and the more disastrous their defeat. The people in other parts of the world will see still more clearly that U.S. imperialism can be defeated, and that what the Vietnamese people can do, they can do too.

History has proved and will go on proving that people's war is the most effective weapon against U.S. imperialism and its lackeys. All revolutionary people will learn to wage people's war against U.S. imperialism and its lackeys. They will take up arms, learn to fight battles and become skilled in waging people's war, though they have not done so before. U.S. imperialism, like a mad bull dashing from place to place, will finally be burned to ashes in the blazing fires of the people's wars it has provoked by its own actions.

Détente

Editor's Introduction: Lin Piao in his statement calls for violent revolution around the world, as Bundy charged. But nowhere does he call for Chinese conquest or domination. People's wars, by definition, are fought by the native population. But however much Bundy exaggerated Chinese aggressive intentions, there is no question that the Chinese statement is belligerent and not designed to curry favor with the government of the United States.

What happened to change this hostile situation and make the Nixon visit and better relations between the two countries possible?

First of all, the United States began to pull its ground troops out of Indochina so that China no longer feared an invasion from the south. The United States, for its part, recognized that the Chinese were not out to conquer the world.

Second, the United States was willing to state that the future of the island of Taiwan (Formosa) was exclusively a Chinese affair. Taiwan is the island off the China coast to which Chiang K'ai-shek fled after his government was defeated by the Communists in 1949. Chiang's continuing presence there was made possible only by U.S. military forces and supplies. And long after the defeat of Chiang's government on the China mainland, the United States and a number of other governments continued to recognize it as the only

Joint Communiqué (Peking: Foreign Language Press, March, 1972).

China's gift of giant panda bears to the United States in 1972 symbolized a new, friendlier relationship.

legitimate government of China. America's promise to withdraw its troops was a major step toward improved relations.

A third and probably the most important reason for improved U.S.–China relations was the rapidly deteriorating relationship between China and the U.S.S.R. America's fear of a Chinese-Russian alliance in 1949 was one of the major factors shaping our policy toward China. It has now become clear that China and the U.S.S.R. fear each other more than either fears the United States. When in the early 1970's China perceived the danger of a war with Russia, she had reason to try to improve relations with the United States to prevent a two-front war.

For these and other reasons, Chinese and American statements about each other have lately been rather moderate. The basis for improved relations is set forth in the joint communiqué that was issued at the conclusion of President Nixon's visit to China in February, 1972.

In what respects does it differ from the two statements you read earlier?⤳

PRESIDENT RICHARD NIXON of the United States of America visited the People's Republic of China at the invitation of Premier Chou En-lai of the People's Republic of China from February 21 to February 28, 1972. Accompanying the President were Mrs. Nixon, U.S. Secretary of State William Rogers, Assistant to the President Dr. Henry Kissinger, and other American officials.

President Nixon met with Chairman Mao Tse-tung of the Communist Party of China on February 21. The two leaders had a serious and frank exchange of views on Sino-U.S. relations and world affairs. . . .

The leaders of the People's Republic of China and the United States of America found it beneficial to have this opportunity, after so many years without contact, to present candidly to one another their views on a variety of issues. They reviewed the international situation in which important changes and great upheavals are taking place and expounded their respective positions and attitudes.

The Chinese side stated: Wherever there is oppression, there is resistance. Countries want independence, nations want liberation, and the people want revolution—this has become the irresistible trend of history. All nations, big or small, should be equal; big nations should not bully the small and strong nations should not bully the weak. China will never be a superpower and it opposes hegemony and power politics of any kind. The Chinese side stated that it firmly supports the struggles of all the oppressed people and nations for freedom and liberation and that the people of all countries have the right to choose their social systems according to their own wishes and the right to safeguard the independence, sovereignty, and territorial integrity of their own countries and oppose foreign aggression, interference, control, and subversion. All foreign troops should be withdrawn to their own countries. . . .

The U.S. side stated: Peace in Asia and peace in the world

requires efforts both to reduce immediate tensions and to eliminate the basic causes of conflict. The United States will work for a just and secure peace: just, because it fulfills the aspirations of peoples and nations for freedom and progress; secure, because it removes the danger of foreign aggression. The United States supports individual freedom and social progress for all the peoples of the world, free of outside pressure or intervention. The United States believes that the effort to reduce tensions is served by improving communication between countries that have different ideologies, so as to lessen the risks of confrontation through accident, miscalculation, or misunderstanding. Countries should treat each other with mutual respect and be willing to compete peacefully, letting performance be the ultimate judge. No country should claim infallibility and each country should be prepared to re-examine its own attitudes for the common good. . . .

There are essential differences between China and the United States in their social systems and foreign policies. However, the two sides agreed that countries, regardless of their social systems, should conduct their relations on the principles of respect for the sovereignty and territorial integrity of all states, nonaggression against other states, noninterference in the internal affairs of other states, equality and mutual benefit, and peaceful coexistence. International disputes should be settled on this basis, without resorting to the use or threat of force. The United States and the People's Republic of China are prepared to apply these principles to their mutual relations.

With these principles of international relations in mind the two sides stated that:

—progress toward the normalization of relations between China and the United States is in the interests of all countries;

—both wish to reduce the danger of international military conflict;

—neither should seek hegemony in the Asia-Pacific region and each is opposed to efforts by any other country or group of countries to establish such hegemony; and

—neither is prepared to negotiate on behalf of any third

party or to enter into agreements or understandings with the other directed at other states.

Both sides are of the view that it would be against the interests of the peoples of the world for any major country to collude with another against other countries, or for major countries to divide up the world into spheres of interest.

The two sides reviewed the long-standing serious disputes between China and the United States. The Chinese side re-affirmed its position: The Taiwan question is the crucial question obstructing the normalization of relations between China and the United States; the Government of the People's Republic of China is the sole legal government of China; Taiwan is a province of China which has long been returned to the motherland; the liberation of Taiwan is China's internal affair in which no other country has the right to interfere; and all U.S. forces and military installations must be withdrawn from Taiwan. The Chinese Government firmly opposes any activities that aim at the creation of "one China, one Taiwan," "one China, two governments," "two Chinas," an "independent Taiwan" or advocate that "the status of Taiwan remains to be determined."

The U.S. side declared: The United States acknowledges that all Chinese on either side of the Taiwan Strait maintain there is but one China and that Taiwan is a part of China. The United States Government does not challenge that position. It reaffirms its interest in a peaceful settlement of the Taiwan question by the Chinese themselves. With this prospect in mind, it affirms the ultimate objective of the withdrawal of all U.S. forces and military installations from Taiwan. In the meantime, it will progressively reduce its forces and military installations on Taiwan as the tension in the area diminishes.

The two sides agreed that it is desirable to broaden the understanding between the two peoples. To this end, they discussed specific areas in such fields as science, technology, culture, sports, and journalism, in which people-to-people contacts and exchanges would be mutually beneficial. Each side undertakes to facilitate the further development of such contacts and exchanges.

Both sides view bilateral trade as another area from which mutual benefit can be derived, and agreed that economic relations based on equality and mutual benefit are in the interest of the peoples of the two countries. They agree to facilitate the progressive development of trade between their two countries.

The two sides agreed that they will stay in contact through various channels, including the sending of a senior U.S. representative to Peking from time to time for concrete consulta-

Chairman Mao Tse-tung and President Nixon meet on the afternoon of February 21, 1972.

tions to further the normalization of relations between the two countries and continue to exchange views on issues of common interest.

The two sides expressed the hope that the gains achieved during this visit would open up new prospects for the relations between the two countries. They believe that the normalization of relations between the two countries is not only in the interest of the Chinese and American peoples but also contributes to the relaxation of tension in Asia and the world.

President Nixon, Mrs. Nixon, and the American party expressed their appreciation for the gracious hospitality shown them by the Government and people of the People's Republic of China.

Editor's Postscript: Trade and diplomatic relations developed slowly following the Shanghai Communique. Formal diplomatic recognition, with exchange of ambassadors, was not achieved until 1979, under President Carter. But mutual interests in both domestic and foreign affairs have contributed to a steady growth in the relationship.

Postscript: America
Through Chinese Eyes

❧§*Editor's Introduction:* Thus far we have viewed China through Chinese eyes. Let us now use the same lens to look at ourselves. How does America appear through the eyes of Chinese Americans? Obviously perceptions vary. But all Chinese Americans share the experience of being an ethnic and racial minority in America. What can we learn about ourselves from them?

Like other groups of immigrants—the Irish, for example—large numbers of Chinese first came to the United States in the mid-nineteenth century to work in the gold mines, help build the railroads, and open up new land. Most of these "coolie" laborers were peasants lured to America by the prospect of earning enough money to break out of the poverty that oppressed their families at home.

At first the Chinese were welcomed in the United States. The demand for labor was great in the newly opened American West, and the Chinese were willing to do jobs that were unpopular with white men who were less financially pressed. But after the transcontinental railroad was completed in 1869, and as more and more people moved to California, attitudes toward Chinese immigrants began to change. Many Americans wanted to drive the Chinese out. Jobs were hard to find, and many employers preferred hiring Chinese to other laborers. The reason for this is evident in the testimony of a factory proprietor at a U.S. Senate hearing on Chinese immigration. He said he had to pay white male adults $2.25 to $5.00 a day, white children $1.00 a day, and "young Chinamen" only $.90 a day. He added that the Chinese were steadier and more reliable than young whites. Other manufacturers testified that they would have to close up if they could not hire cheap Chinese labor.

Chinese were also used as "scabs" on strikebreakers to counter the efforts of white laborers to organize for higher wages and better working conditions. The result was often mob violence with strong racist overtones. Riots, beatings, and lynchings became com-

monplace occurrences wherever Chinese were employed. Hatred
and fear of Chinese finally resulted in the Exclusion Act of 1882
and other racially discriminatory legislation designed not only to
prevent further Chinese immigration but gradually to eliminate

*Chinese coolies working on a railroad in the American West in the
nineteenth century. (From D. E. Fehrenbacher and N. E. Tutorow,
California, An Illustrated History, New York: Van Nostrand, 1968,
p. 70.)*

the Chinese from America altogether. Many Chinese departed the country, and most of those who remained were driven into ghettos. The readings that follow are taken from interviews conducted in the largest of these ghettos, San Francisco's Chinatown.

Over the years, attitudes have changed, as has the situation of people of Chinese lineage living in America. Immigration prohibitions were lifted long ago, and, of course, many Chinese no longer live in Chinatowns. A striking example of the difference between generations is apparent in the 1960 census figures for California, which reveal that Chinese Americans had both the highest percentage of college graduates and the highest percentage of illiterates of any ethnic group in the state.

The readings that follow provide a small but diverse sample of life in the United States for Chinese Americans. The speakers are a successful businessman, a working woman, a high school student, and a prizewinning author and playwright.&

The Americanization of Johnny Kan

&*Editor's Introduction:* Many Chinese who stayed in America after the Exclusion Act surmounted race prejudice and became successful by American standards. Such was the case of Johnny Kan, who established a luxury restaurant in San Francisco's Chinatown in the 1930s. How did Johnny Kan become successful? How do his attitudes differ from those of his older Chinese partners?&

WE HAD A very difficult time growing up. At one time there had been over two thousand Chinese living in Grass Valley and working in the gold mines. But by the time we got up there it had dwindled down to a few hundred. A lot of the men had fallen back on vegetable peddling. . . . You know, it was a rough bunch of characters who came to California to the Mother Lode, and they would treat Chinese as inferior and stone them because we looked different and acted different. So they used to stone the vegetable peddlers, . . . they used to throw stones at us on the way home. Oh, they would wrap rocks in snowballs and throw them at us. Of course, children

Victor G. Nee and Brett de Bary Nee, *Longtime Californ': A Documentary Study of an American Chinatown* (New York: Pantheon, 1973), pp. 110–16, abridged.

we must forgive, because they were innocent, but at that time it was a very confusing thing for me. . . . [W]hen I was nineteen . . . I was working at a grocery called Sam Hing and Company. . . .

I remember we had an old sign on the window and it wasn't attractive. I wanted to create a better image with a better designed sign and matching stationery and business cards to indicate what we had for sale. So as a partner and assistant manager of the store, as well as the *Choot Fonn*—the English secretary—I took it upon myself to have the sign changed. Now my oldtimer partners in this store had been picking on me a lot, saying we American-born were lazy, we weren't fluent in Chinese, *"Tow-gee jai mo no,* the American-born have no brains." I knew it would be useless to try to discuss my ideas about the sign with them, so I just went ahead and had it done. At the time, nobody said a thing. They barely seemed to notice the change. But at the end of the year, when they were ready to pay out our small dividends, I got hauled in on the sign.

They said, "Now you're taking too much for granted. You're making expenditures without the approval of the rest of the partners." I told them I had thought it was just in the line of duty to repair that sign, to improve the business, and to make progress. . . . But they said, "No, everybody should be consulted. In China, the older the sign, the more venerable and reputable the business is. You have destroyed and taken away . . . our symbol of being long-established." And I said, "Well, this is not China, this is America. And all over the world business people are changing their ideas and their trademarks."

The old sign had said something like this: "SAM HING & CO., Groceries and Peanuts." I had changed it to a better script, and underneath the top line, "SAM HING & CO., Grocers," I put another line "Wholesalers in Peanuts." I thought this was important because . . . it made it clear that our peanut business was in the wholesale class, it wasn't just a store that sold bags of peanuts. Fortunately, something happened to prove me right. A few weeks later my brother, who was between jobs, came to the store to help out and catch some meals. He asked me, "Why don't you advertise in something like *Variety* magazine, or *Show Business* magazine?" I said, "What good will that do?" He said, "You dumb cluck, the circus people read it, too!" So I went and bought a small ad in *Variety*.

Months later a man walked into Sam Hing's and said, "Let me try some of your peanuts." We brought him samples, . . . quoted a price, and finally he chose a brand. He said, "Can you deliver two tons by tomorrow morning?" Two tons! That was practically our whole stock! It turned out this man was a buyer from Ringling Brothers. I was about to tell him it was impossible when my brother started shouting in my ear, "Take it! Everybody roasts peanuts all night long!" So we worked all night and we got the order out. In the morning we drove it, ten sacks at a time, to the circus grounds in our little truck. We shoveled all the peanuts into the big circus trucks, and they sold so well they asked us to come back every day. At the end of the year, when my partners had made such a fuss about that sign, I told them to deduct forty dollars from my salary. But after this order came in, I got my forty dollars back pretty fast.

After working at Sam Hing's for eight years, I still didn't see eye to eye with my partners on progress. I thought we should convert the grocery department into a self-service operation, they kept holding back, so finally I left and went to L.A. for a while. When I came back, things were not good in San Francisco in the thirties, and I had to do all kinds of things, janitorial work, dishwashing, cooking, anything to get started again. . . .

Well, by the thirties Chinatown was already becoming a neon-sign salesman's dream with every shop competing for space and gaudiness. I began talking with some friends and joined a little project to restore "Old Chinatown." Our aim was to bring back the old jewelry, slipper, and lantern-manufacturing shops, to make it look like Chinatown before the earthquake and fire, no neon signs, no jazzy commercial appearance. Unfortunately, due to mismanagement, the project flopped. But then I began thinking about something else. I

thought back on the success of the Chinese restaurateurs in
New York and Chicago in the roaring twenties. They were
. . . packing in four to five hundred customers at one seating
on Saturday nights. These were the restaurants where many
big names in the band business started out—people like Paul
Whiteman, Kay Kyser, Paul Tremaine. You know, Chinese
from San Francisco would willingly go to New York or Chicago just to work as waiters in these places. The crowds were
so large and the tips so good, they wouldn't even ask for sal-
aries!

Also, I had studied the old Mandarin Restaurant here on
Bush Street and figured out why it had failed. First, for lack of
professional restaurant experience, and second, because it had
too many partners—a lethal combination! And finally I realized
that the reason there were no first-class restaurants in Chinatown was because no one ever bothered to study, and to teach
their employees, how to run a really fine place. And nobody
had tried to educate Caucasians to an appreciation of Chinese
food. There were over fifty restaurants in Chinatown—papa-
mama, medium-sized, juke and soup joints, tenderloin joints,
and others—where the waiters just slammed the dishes on the
table and cared less about the customer or what he wanted to
eat.

So we decided to launch the first efficiency operated . . .
Chinese restaurant. Our concept was to have a Ming or Tang
dynasty theme for decor, a fine crew of master chefs, and a
well-organized dining-room crew headed by a courteous maître
d', host, hostesses, and so on. And we topped it all off with a
glass-enclosed kitchen. This would serve many purposes. The
customers could actually see Chinese food being prepared, and
it would encourage everybody to keep the kitchen clean. Also,
in those hectic pioneering times, in a party of six or eight persons, there would always be one who disliked Chinese food.
No matter what the captain or waiters may say to him, his
answer is, "I hate Chinese food, bring me a steak!" Then what?

Well, with our glass-enclosed kitchen, we could say to the
difficult guest, "Will you please do us a favor! Come and watch

us prepare fresh food and see our *woks* [cooking pans]." It usually took me about fifteen minutes to educate a disliker when I could have him smell the aroma of fresh, barbecued pork coming out of the oven, or sizzling filet of chicken . . . with beautiful, fresh vegetables toss-cooked for just a few seconds. Usually a man like this will end up being a real enthusiast. Why? Because he never knew how real Chinese food was prepared. Now he was no longer a chop suey believer. And of course, in the years since that initial education period, we've introduced our friends to . . . many complex dishes enjoyed by Cantonese people. . . .

Chinese children in nineteenth-century America. (From William Bronson, The Earth Shook, the Sky Burned, *Garden City, New York: Doubleday, 1959.)*

I guess I'd say what kept me going in this business, even when there were all the setbacks, was the sense that there was such great potential in it if people are properly trained. I think the restaurant business is something like show business. Now back stage, the chefs may be sweating and arguing with the waiters, and the waiters are arguing with the busboys, and everything is clanging away. But when they come out to the dining room everyone smiles. The maître d' greets you, the waiter bows, the cocktail girls are very gracious. It's what they call being a trooper, you see. . . .

The Exploitation of Jennie Lew

≈§Editor's Introduction: With the expansion of the American economy following World War II, many Chinese began moving out of Chinatowns and entering professional and white-collar jobs. According to the Nees, California's 1960 census figures "attributed to American Chinese both the highest percentage of college-educated and the highest percentage of near-illiterate population of any ethnic group in the state."

Even for the highly trained and educated Chinese, however, a lingering racial prejudice often kept them from rising above middle-level jobs. For recent immigrants, the situation has often been far worse, as the following account indicates. What conditions contributed to the exploitation of Jennie Lew? Is hers a case of racial discrimination? How does she find relief?§≈

JENNIE TALKS TO us with her oldest daughter, a thin and nervous girl of twenty, and two boys in the room. She says she began working in the garment factories about fifteen years ago, when Donna got old enough to keep an eye on the younger ones. Of course, she worked off and on, she says. She'd stop for four or five months whenever a new child was born, and her health hasn't been too good, so she had to take time out for that. In all, she worked in three different garment factories until she stopped. She had worked in the last place, on Powell Street, for seven years, making men's shirts. . . .

She followed pretty much the same schedule every day while she was working. She'd get up at seven and make breakfast for her husband and the kids. She'd walk the older ones to school, go to the factory at nine, and work for two hours. . . . At eleven, she'd pick the kids up from school, make lunch for them at home, walk them back to school, and be at work again at one. At five, she would take another hour off to cook

Nee and Nee, *op. cit.*, pp. 290–95, abridged.

supper for everybody. At six or six-thirty she'd go back to work again, sew until ten, then come home to bed. On Saturday she would put in about five hours and take home something to sew on Sunday. She was paid by piece-rate, not by the hour, earning between $4.50 to $8 per dozen, depending on the complexity of the pattern.

We ask Jennie what the shop was like and she says . . . there were about thirty machines in the shop. It was noisy because there were so many people running motors, but the main thing is that it was messy: an old building, no one painted or dusted the walls. . . .

Jennie says she didn't expect to do work like this when she was a girl. In fact, she never liked sewing. "But that's the only thing we know how to do when we get here. It's the only kind of job we can get." Donna says Jennie is impatient and she used to scream at them sometimes when she got fed up with sewing. . . . "After a while, we just turn off on it when she starts yelling like that. You get the feeling she couldn't control anything about her life, and it makes you feel awful.". . .

Jennie had always been paid by piece-rate, but in the years since she had begun at Powell Street, the effort to unionize the Chinatown shops had intensified. Chinatown wage levels had been exposed and become the center of a bitter, city-wide controversy.

In 1963, when she began working for him, Kim Wah Lee informed her that a prerequisite for maintaining her position as a worker at his shop would be that she, like the other workers, fill out a biweekly time card certifying that her wages came up to the standard for the state minimum wage of $1.65 per hour. He instructed the women in the following procedure: as before, their wages would be piece-rate, calculated according to the number of pieces completed, not the number of hours worked. They would, as before, hand in a slip for every dozen garments completed. But at the end of every two-week period, Kim Wah Lee would give them a separate time card to take home and fill out, showing, as federal law requires, not the number of pieces completed, but the number of hours worked. With each time card, he would enclose a brief note of instruction stating precisely the number of hours to be filled in on the time card. The number was, of course, not calculated on the basis of a record of actual hours worked, but by dividing the actual amount the woman had earned by the state minimum wage. If she worked eighty hours and earned fifty dollars in two weeks, she was instructed to fill out the time card to show a total of no more than 30 hours, at which rate her pay for the two-week period would appear to fulfill the minimum wage of $1.65 per hour.

Jennie said for a while she didn't understand why she was being asked to do this. After a few months, her husband noticed her working out figures on the card every two weeks. He began to blow up whenever she brought the time card home. . . . "You're not supposed to fill in your own time card!" He urged her to quit and look for another job. But she was convinced she couldn't find work outside of the garment industry, and she needed money. She and most of the other women were aware they were being cheated. "That was obvious, but what could we do? Most of us can't speak English. Even if a few of us wanted to start something, like file a petition, we couldn't get support from the others. People are hesitant about starting anything, because they can lose their positions so easily. So no one wants to stir things up, you know.". . .

In the summer of 1968, Jennie began going to the North Beach health clinic complaining of dizzy spells, headaches, backaches, and general fatigue. Her health deteriorated through the fall and winter, and in the following spring the doctor advised her to stop work for an indefinite period of time. Because she was anxious about losing . . . income, Jennie hesitated for several months. . . . In late June, Jennie developed mononucleosis and was hospitalized for three weeks. She took sick leave from work for another month.

In August, when she decided to apply for unemployment insurance, she was told that she needed a letter from her employer stating the reason for her inability to continue work. Jennie took the form to the shop. Her boss refused to sign it and told her her sickness was all in her head. Jennie says she exploded. "There's no other way to explain what happened. I was just fed up. Before I even thought about what I was saying, I told him if he didn't fill out that card for me, I would sue him for all the hours he'd never paid me in four years. He just said, 'Go right ahead,' and told me to leave the shop." Jennie went home and collected the receipts of the paychecks she had received in the year period before she had to leave work. In the period between August 19, 1967, and June 22, 1968, she earned $969.00.

It was difficult to get Jennie to explain the steps which led her to become the first garment worker in Chinatown history who successfully won a court battle against her employer in 1971. She says it was not her husband's pressure which led to the decision, it was just the rage that built up in herself. . . . She went to the Economic Opportunity Office on Stockton Street, where she had learned to come for food stamps, and someone on the staff advised her to discuss her case with the ILGWU (International Ladies Garment Workers Union) office on Howard Street. The union urged Jennie to prosecute the case, and referred her to the Chinatown–North Beach Neighborhood Legal Assistance Office. For two years, Jennie and a young lawyer in the office put together the evidence on the case. Jennie was able to produce several time cards, with the usual biweekly instructions on them; these became critical evidence in the case. Neither her lawyer nor Jennie was able to obtain the agreement of any other women in the shop to testify in court. Jennie's two youngest children, however, were able to provide evidence of overtime work by giving the hours of the day and the times of the week when their mother was away from home.

The lawyer stressed that he felt legal blame for Jennie's experience did not rest only on the proprietor of her shop. "Legally, this Chinese contractor . . . was merely an extension of the manufacturing company downtown.". . . He says he approached the downtown firm about the case, but they were so anxious to keep it out of court and out of the public eye that they offered to settle all expenses themselves. Since he felt the success of a court case might be one of the biggest breakthroughs possible for workers in the Chinatown industry, he and Jennie went on to court. After seven months they won a settlement. Jennie received $2,100 in back pay for the five-year period, plus a $1,650 punitive fee which was imposed on her employer.

In the spring of 1970, when she was well enough to look for work again, Jennie found a new job. She is now a maid in a large hotel . . . outside Chinatown. It's hard work, she has to get up even earlier now to be down there on time. But her work hours are a regular forty-hour week, the pay is $2.25 an hour, and she has a paid two-week vacation and sick leave. Jennie says she would never work in the garment factory again.

The Politicization of Clifford Fong

❧*Editor's Introduction:* The next selection, by a high school student, reveals a new attitude that has arisen among many young Chinese Americans since the mid-1960s. What does Clifford Fong see as the reason for Chinese American problems? Does he have a solution?❧

ONE OF THE biggest problems we used to have, you know, was that the white man didn't recognize us as having any problems at all. Because, like we have some of the best restaurants in the city here, we have fancy shops, we have bus tours going through here, you know. There's no bus tours going through Harlem or Watts. Because the people, even the outside white people, know what's happening down there, what they read and what they see on TV has a lot to do with it. But what they read and what they see on TV about Chinatown, you know, it's a clean place where everybody's happy, and there's no trouble. And that means a lot of people are getting screwed up down here and don't receive no help. So that was, you know, one of the biggest jobs. Just to let the outside people know what's happening.

Like the tourists, tourists in Chinatown are important for all the money, but it's just that the money don't benefit all the

Nee and Nee, *op. cit.,* pp. 345–48, abridged.

people. It benefits the businesses, see. You know, if you're rich, you're very rich, if you're poor, it just keeps on going like that. I think the tourists come in to use, to take advantage of the way Chinatown is set up. You know, it's cheaper than other places and even the so-called white hippies can afford to come down. Like they made this, I don't know, one of the hippie papers made this pamphlet "How to Live in San Francisco" and they list a lot of Chinatown restaurants, the cheapest place you can go for a good meal. So a lot of tourists just come down and they expect the Chinese to wait on them, serve them hand and foot. They expect all the Chinese to be what they see in the magazines and the cartoons, you know. . . .

It used to be humble, docile, you know, hardworking, industrious, you know, little man that never starts any trouble. The white man looks upon the Chinese as very humble, a short little guy with buck tooth, glasses, round thick glasses or something like that. Isn't masculine at all as far as the guys are concerned. And they all like to work hard, never start no trouble. And I guess in San Francisco things are a little bit more liberal, but maybe in the Midwest or the South there are some people that never saw a Chinese in their whole life. Or some kids that only saw Chinese on TV where we acted as butlers, waiters, houseboys. Even in the movies that were made on the Chinese, or the Japanese war movies, like there's the white American sergeant six feet tall, you know, John Wayne type, and then the little Japanese soldiers so small that ten of them couldn't take on John Wayne even though they all got guns. And that's all the white man sees. Well, like I said, last year we begin speaking up a little bit more and maybe in San Francisco at least maybe white people are awakening a little bit.

As far as a lot of the youth is concerned, when the tourists come down they expect us to act like our stereotype, especially the youth. Cause we're supposed to be well behaved and everything. And then when they see all the so-called juvenile delinquents standing on Jackson Street, you know, they're shocked. Because a lot of tourists think they can come down and take advantage of our humbleness and stupidity in being docile, never defending ourselves, and especially like the guys being unmasculine and everything, and they think they can get away with pushing the Chinese around and they'll never fight back. That's why a lot of these tourists come down here and when they get wise or something then the street kids get in trouble with them. You know, they're real resentful of any white man who would take advantage of them. So that's why a lot of white men get their ass kicked when they come down. . . .

Because I think like the main thing is the economic exploitation of all the people, you know. Especially when it comes to Chinese because again that stereotype of we're supposed to work hard and keep our mouths shut and it doesn't matter what you get paid. A lot of white businessmen take advantage of this. Richer Chinese take advantage of poor Chinese. Even if a guy owns a restaurant making thousands of dollars, he'll still pay that dishwasher fifty cents an hour. Which goes back to the old thing they say in China, the plain greed of the businessman. Why not if you can get away with it? Why pay the guy a dollar if he takes fifty cents? So that's why a lot of people are suffering in Chinatown and a lot of people are getting rich, too.

Well, you know, whenever I talk about white as exploiting and all that I don't mean the white race, I mean white America. That's a pretty big difference to me. And you know it's not a lot of white people doing the exploiting and everything, but as far as I'm concerned all white people are to blame because all white people are ignorant of the things that are going on. And if you're ignorant you don't care what's happening. There are a lot of poor whites that are getting ripped off, too, in this country, that's true. But this is a pretty rich country, so in the end a lot of it has to do with our race. A poor white will get work easier than a poor black or an immigrant just because of the color of the skin. . . .

Yeah, I think a lot of what's going on back in China. I think communism is good for that country, China. Because when they had kings and all that, or when the Nationalists were running the country, the majority of the people were suffering. I think Mao's government is helping out the people more and that's good. But that doesn't necessarily mean that communism will work here. It's a different thing altogether, people think differently, live differently. So it's good for China, but you can't say it's good for the United States.

An Emerging Chinese-American Sensibility

◈§Editor's Introduction: Our final selection is an interview with Frank Chin, a writer whose works have appeared in numerous magazines and anthologies and who won an award for his play *Chickencoop Chinaman.*

In the first part of the interview Chin is describing an experience in Iowa, where he was a Fellow at the State University. What does Frank Chin realize about himself and other Chinese Americans? What is the significance of the incident with his father? What does he see as his role in life?§◈

EVERYONE THERE treated me like a foreigner, including the Chinese students, because I was a foreigner to them, and that got very depressing. The only place I could get a job was in the Chinese restaurant in this town. Getting a place to live, well, this professor befriended me, found me a room, and took me over to see the landlady. The landlady came out and I was smoking. The guy said, "You better put your cigarette out, she might not approve." I'd just started the cigarette so I bent over, pinched it out, and I was putting it back in my pocket, kind of hunched over, and I look up, this lady is bowing to me. I look at the professor, he kind of shrugs, so I bow, and he bows.

She says, "Is this him?" "Yes, this is Frank Chin and this is Mrs. So and So." I say, "How do you do, Mrs. So and So." She says, "Oh, he speaks English!" "Yes, I do, Mrs. So and So." She says, "What's his name?" "My name is Frank, ma'am." "Oh, well, that's only your American name." And I had to admit that's probably all it was, you know. "Yeah, it's only my American name." And I'm getting really tired of this. Then she says, "You speak very fluent English!" "Thank you, ma'am." "Oh, what part of China are you from?"

"I'm from San Francisco, ma'am." Rather than put her

Nee and Nee, *op. cit.*, pp. 380–89, abridged.

down and say, "You dumb bitch, I'm not from China." But she goes on, "How long have you been in this country?" You know, that was her mental set: all Chinese are foreigners, therefore San Francisco is in China. I said, "Well, I've been here twenty years or so." And she said, "You should speak good English, then!" And I said, "Yes, I should, shouldn't I?"

She took me to one end of the room. "Do you like this rug?" "No, I don't like this rug." "That rug okay?" "Yeah, that rug's okay." She said, "Are you going to do any cooking?" I said, "Yeah, I've been known to do a little cooking so I can eat every now and again." She said, "All right, I'll bring you some things. I know, Chinese like to make a mess when they cook, don't they?" I said no, I didn't know that. She said, "Oh, yes, I've been to the Philippines and I know that when Chinese cook they like to have a big mess. I'll just bring you some cloth to wipe off the stove each time you cook." I said, "O.K. You bring me the cloth and I'll wipe the stove with it. Gladly, gladly." She says, "Well, here we call it 'rags.' " "Oh, 'rags.' Cu-lean-ing rrrrags." "Excuse me. Cu-lean-ing rrrrags." I'm looking at her and she's staring me in the face, mouthing the words "cleaning rags," and I realize I'm being given a lesson in English. . . .

But the thing taught me something, you know. That I was Chinese-American, whatever that meant. That I was not an individual, not just a human being. A human being in this culture, in this society, is a white man, he can disappear. I couldn't disappear, no matter how enlightened I was, no matter how straight my English was. Someone, just because they saw my skin color, would detect an accent. Someone would always correct me. And well, then I began to look at my writing, what I'd been writing about in my letters and everything was just to this point. The Chinese-American, well, schizophrenia. That I'd been playing a kind of ping-pong game, you know. Now I'm Chinese, now I'm American. But up against real Chinese in this isolated setting I saw that I had nothing in common with them. That they didn't understand me, and I didn't understand them. We both used chopsticks, okay, that's recognizable. But that's mechanics, not culture. On a personal gut level that doesn't make us brothers. . . .

What I value most, I guess, is what I'm doing, trying to legitimize the Chinese-American sensibility. Call it my accident in time and space and that all the talent, everything I have is good only for this. Nothing else is any good until I get this done or started. And if I can't legitimize it, or if Chinese-American sensibility isn't legitimized, then my writing is no good. . . .

Deep down I really don't think anything's going to come of this. I think I'll end up like a certain relative of mine, looked on as a bum by my family, selling newspapers on the corner of Grant and Washington. Like, you know, the only

The diabolical Chinese, from the MGM film "Mr. Wu" (1927). (From Harold Isaacs, Scratches on Our Minds, *New York: John Day, 1958, p. 240.)*

choice I see for me is, well, am I going to be a bum in Chinatown or outside of Chinatown?

In my family, and among Chinese, the question of just physical survival is almost of paramount importance. How do you live? By their terms I'll never grow up, I'll never make a lot of money. I know I'd feel a lot worse if I took some crummy job and gave up my writing, because I've tried that, and it just did not work. At the same time this is my sense of guilt, that I do feel bad when my family looks on me as a failure, that I disgust them. That as far as they're concerned I'm some sort of weirdo charity case. And even if I succeed, I will have failed them.

I identify with my father. My father tried, in his own way he tried as hard as I am to make it in his terms in this country. Yeah, I think he failed and I think he thinks he's failed. But in his eyes I'm irresponsible. I'm fooling around and I'm an insult to him. He was president of the Six Companies, I've insulted him there. There was one time I came down from Seattle, you know, I was dressed just like this but he loves me, I'm his son, and he took me out to get some clams. He knows I love clams. And we were at *Sun Tōi Sam Yuen* on Jackson Street and a bunch of his buddies were there. We were in a booth, and I had long, long hair then. They recognized him but they didn't see me. So they came over, shook hands with him, said a few words. But when they saw me they wouldn't acknowledge me, didn't even ask who I was. Before, when I was a little neater they would say something, or shake my hand. But they didn't acknowledge me, and I saw my father die. And there's nothing I can do for the guy. I felt terrible for him, I was breaking his heart. I guess for him it was a very noble moment, do or die maintaining himself as my father even though it meant insult. So they came by, and the wives came by one at a time and there I was with my pile of clams.

We live in different worlds. And when my world comes in contact with his we just destroy each other. I look at the way he tunes the television set, it's all wrong. The people look like they're dead. They come on looking dingy, gray, the color of Roquefort cheese. But that's the way he sees the world. And he lives in Chinatown, so it's in Chinatown, his world. And he can't see that it's partly my world, too. So, you know, I'll never have his respect. And I could win a Nobel . . . prize, you know, and prove that my writing's been worthwhile and he'll say, "You dress like a bum." And then I see that I've broken the guy's heart. So I feel bad about that.

Asian Students: A Success Story

Editor's Introduction: The experiences of Chinese-Americans, like the experiences of all immigrant groups in the U.S., have undergone changes over time. The blatant discrimination against Jennie Lew, or the sense of alienation of Clifford Fong, or the feeling of Frank Chin that he was a failure in his father's eyes are not typical of most young Chinese-Americans today. Indeed, Chinese-American students, as well as children of Korean and Japanese parents, are doing extremely well by any standards.

   The following selection, written in 1981, describes the high school academic performance of Asian-American students in the Washington, D.C. area and nationwide. What accounts for the success of these students? What role does their parents' traditional culture play in this success?

   Although his mother speaks to him mostly in Korean, she taught him how to read in English when he was only 4.

   By the time he reached junior high, while other boys played after school, he usually studied or practiced the piano.

   Last month Victor You, 17, whose parents come from Korea, graduated as valedictorian from the selective St. Albans School in Northwest Washington, D.C. He had the highest grades in his class, took four college-level courses, won the school's music award, and was a National Merit

Lawrence Feinberg, "Asian Students Excelling in Area, U.S. Schools,"*The Washington Post,* July 12, 1981. © 1981 by The Washington Post Company. Reprinted by permission.

Scholarship finalist. This fall he is heading to Harvard University.

"My parents always taught us to excel so we would never be in the position of being bossed around," You said. "We know we are a minority in this country, and we have to do better than other Americans. . . . That's the only way we'll get ahead."

At Anacostia High School, where virtually all students are black and poor in contrast to St. Albans, where most are white and well-to-do, this year's valedictorian is also Asian American, Chin Wah Lee, 17, who was born in Hong Kong.

"In Asia a scholar is revered," Lee said, "and my parents felt I should do well in school. That's the only way to get ahead . . . . It seems like a lot of students have a sense of apathy toward schoolwork. They don't seem to care. [But] when you first come over there is a need to prove you can succeed. People who are born here don't have that need anymore."

You and Lee—their schools sharply different, their drive almost the same—are part of a widespread pattern of Asian students doing exceptionally well both locally and across the country.

Even though Asians are a minority of less than 3 percent in the Washington area, Asian names cropped up often on this spring's lists of top-ranking local high school graduates.

On standardized tests in Montgomery County, Maryland, Asians scored higher than any racial group. Their composite scores last year were slightly above whites in every grade tested.

Nationally, in a major survey of high school students sponsored by the U.S. Education Department, Asians had far higher scores in mathematics than any other group, including whites, blacks, Hispanics and American Indians. Whites were the highest by a smaller margin in reading and vocabulary.

Overall, Asian seniors came out slightly ahead, even though, according to the survey, which was directed by University of Chicago sociologist James Coleman, about 58 percent of the Asian students were foreign born. About 14.5

These students are among the top scholars in the 1981 graduating class at T. C. Williams High School in Alexandria, VA. Although Asians make up only 7 percent of the school's enrollment, four of the top 12 students in the senior class were Asian.

percent were identified as limited English-speaking.

The study also showed that the Asian students did more homework and took more tough courses. Far more of their parents, it reported, expected them to go beyond college for advanced degrees.

"It's a classic story of a group making it through the educational system," said Stephan Thernstrom, a history professor at Harvard and editor of the Harvard Encyclopedia of American Ethnic Groups. "Asians have done well in California schools since the 1930s. Now they're in many more parts of the country, and they're doing well elsewhere too.

"They seem to have an orientation that's attuned to doing

well in American schools . . . . They save. They devote a great deal of attention to their children. They do well."

Of the students admitted to Harvard's freshman class next fall, one of the toughest to get into in the nation, Asian Americans account for 8.9 percent. This is almost six times higher than the proportion of Asians in the American population, which was 1.5 percent in the 1980 census.

At the University of California at Berkeley, 20 percent of undergraduates are of Asian origin, while Asians account for 5.2 percent of California residents. To be eligible for Berkeley students must be in the top 12.5 percent of their high school class. A recent study showed that 39 percent of Asians graduating from California secondary schools did that well, compared with 16.5 percent of whites, 5 percent of blacks, and 4.7 percent of Hispanics.

On a more advanced level, according to a study by the National Academy of Sciences, Asians account for 6.6 percent of all scientists in the United States with doctoral degrees, including 15.5 percent of those in engineering and 9.3 percent in computer science.

"I wish I had a school full of Asian kids," said Anthony Hanley, the principal of T.C. Williams Senior High in Alexandria, Virginia, where Asians make up 7 percent of enrollment but accounted for four of the top 12 students in last month's graduating class. "They're polite. They're hard workers. They're wonderful kids . . . .

"Oh, they're not all perfect always," Hanley continued. "But we've had almost no problems with discipline with them. A lot of the homes are poor. They left everything behind when they came here. But they have this incredible drive to succeed. They're very serious about their studies, and they have a very strong respect for the teachers."

Hanley added that "there is a sense of a little jealousy that these foreigners can just come into the school and after a while they're at the top of the class. It's resented a little. But these Asian kids, they're such workers. They work incredibly hard."

Although the hard work is obvious, exactly why many Asians work so hard in school is uncertain. So are the other reasons underlying their academic success. The main factors cited by historians and sociologists are similar to those given by the students themselves: the high value placed on scholarship in Asian societies, a strong family structure to transmit this value, and the history of discrimination against Asians in the United States, which has caused them to stress education as an open channel to high-status jobs and acceptance.

The same combination of factors is often given to explain the academic success of American Jews, who are also heavily represented on scholastic honors lists and in prestigious universities, said William Petersen, a retired University of California sociologist. Petersen, who wrote a major study of Japanese Americans, said the strong push by Asians to do well in schools now is "fairly comparable to the Jewish drive for excellence, particularly a generation or so ago when many Jews were immigrants and really pushed their kids to excel."

Indeed, a widespread Japanese stereotype with a considerable element of truth, Petersen said, is the *kyoiku-mama*—the "education mama" who is strikingly similar to the stereotyped "Jewish mother," lavishing attention on her children, pushing and helping them to do well in school, and gaining much of her own satisfaction from their success.

"It's a great stereotype," said Harvard's Thernstrom. "And it usually is effective—no matter who uses it."

Although it has lessened recently, discrimination against Asians in the United States often has been severe. On the West Coast, where Asians first settled as "coolie" laborers, farm workers, servants and laundrymen, there was considerable agitation against the "yellow peril," which led to Jim Crow-like laws, Thernstrom said. These served to limit voting, land-holding, and racial intermarriage by Asians. Often their housing was segregated and some communities placed them in segregated schools.

During World War II, 120,000 Japanese-Americans on the West Coast were placed behind barbed wire in internment camps.

The racial prejudice has steeply declined since then,

Thernstrom said, but like blacks, Asians remain a visibly distinct minority and most Asian students interviewed for this article recalled sometimes being taunted by other children, usually with the epithet "chink." In addition, Thernstrom said, many Asians have faced problems with English similar to those of many Hispanics.

Because of discrimination, Asians generally have been placed with blacks, Hispanics and American Indians in affirmative action plans and other special programs for minorities. Yet, unlike the other groups whose test scores, graduation rates, and representation in tough academic programs all are substantially below white averages, Asians have done at least as well as whites in virtually all academic areas.

"It's absurd that Orientals qualify for affirmative action," Thernstrom said, "but it makes the programs work" because Asians generally have strong records. Indeed, at Harvard, which boasts in a house organ that next fall's freshman class has a "record high percentage (22.88) of minority students," slightly more Asian Americans were admitted than blacks even though there are seven times more blacks than Asians in the United States.

At Massachusetts Institute of Technology, which has more than twice as many Asians as blacks, Asians are not included in the school's minority admissions programs. "Asians are not considered to be a minority," MIT news director Robert Byers said. "They are not underrepresented."

Several "minority fellowship programs," sponsored by the National Science Foundation and the National Academy of Sciences, also exclude Asians on the same grounds.

"They don't need it," said one NSF administrator. "They're able to do it on their own. The other people need some more help to make it."

Although Asian organizations have fought hard to keep Asians eligible for minority-preference programs, particularly for government contracts, several of the students interviewed said they did not want their race to be considered in admitting them to college. They added that they thought counting by race might hurt Asians because in proportion to their small numbers there are "too many" Asians in many good universities.

"The colleges sent me all this minority stuff and I felt insulted," said Teresa Chen, who graduated with a straight-A average from High Point Senior High and is going to Brown in the fall. "You get the feeling that they weren't interested in me because I'm me but because I'm a minority . . . They treated me as if I was handicapped. It never occurred to me that I was handicapped because I was Chinese."

In fact, like many of the students interviewed, Chen said she thought being Asian actually helped her do well in school. "My parents are very strict by American standards," she said, "and they really taught us to believe that education is the way to succeed in life. They're proud of the fact that we [Chinese] have been educated and taking tests for thousands of years" for admission to the mandarin class of powerful civil servants.

While they are still a small minority, the number of Asians in the United States grew from 1.5 million to 3.5 million between 1970 and 1980, as the repeal of exclusionary immigration laws allowed the entry of skilled Asian workers, professionals and anticommunist refugees. Most of the newcomers were from Vietnam, China (the People's Republic of China, Taiwan, and Hong Kong), Korea and the Philippines.

Victor You, the valedictorian at St. Albans, said his father is an economist with the World Bank, his mother a chemist who gave up her career to raise two sons. When he was young, he recalled, his mother "would bake a cake every time I read a book to encourage me. I had to do well for her."

Chin Wah Lee, Anacostia's valedictorian, said both his parents work, his father as a cook in a Chinese restaurant, his mother as a dishwasher. Even though the family could clearly use the money, Lee said his parents did not want him to have a job after school. Instead, they encouraged him to take courses at George Washington University while he was still a high school senior, which involved two round trips a day by bus and subway—about three hours of commuting.

"They felt I should do well in school," Lee said, "and spend time studying, not working . . . . They see me as their future. They want me to get ahead."

INDEX

277